Citizen Satisfaction

Citizen Satisfaction

Improving Government Performance, Efficiency, and Citizen Trust

Forrest V. Morgeson III

First published in 2014 by
PALGRAVE MACMILLAN®
in the United States—a division of St. Martin's Press LLC,
175 Fifth Avenue, New York, NY 10010.

Where this book is distributed in the UK, Europe and the rest of the world,
this is by Palgrave Macmillan, a division of Macmillan Publishers Limited,
registered in England, company number 785998, of Houndmills,
Basingstoke, Hampshire RG21 GXS.

Palgrave Macmillan is the global academic imprint of the above companies
and has companies and representatives throughout the world.

Palgrave® and Macmillan® are registered trademarks in the United States,
the United Kingdom, Europe and other countries.

ISBN: 978–0–230–34134–0

Library of Congress Cataloging-in-Publication Data

Morgeson, Forrest V., III.
    Citizen satisfaction : improving government performance, efficiency,
and citizen trust / Forrest V. Morgeson III.
        pages cm
    Includes bibliographical references and index.
    ISBN 978–0–230–34134–0 (hardback)
        1. Public administration—United States—Public opinion. 2. Public
administration—United States—Management. 3. Administrative
agencies—United States—Management. 4. Executive departments—
United States—Management. 5. Government productivity—United
States. 6. Performance—Measurement. 7. Internet in public
administration—United States. I. Title.

JK421.M57 2014
352.8'80973—dc23   2013046990

A catalogue record of the book is available from the British Library.

Design by Newgen Knowledge Works (P) Ltd., Chennai, India.

First edition: May 2014

10 9 8 7 6 5 4 3 2 1

For Claes Fornell, David VanAmburg, and the entire team at ACSI.
You will find many of your own ideas reflected in these pages.
I hope that I have represented them accurately.

Contents

Figures

Tables

Abbreviations

ACSI	American Customer Satisfaction Index
ASQ	American Society for Quality
CATI	computer-assisted telephone interviewing
CFO	Chief Financial Officer
CI	confidence interval
CPI	cost per interview
CSR	customer service representative
EGA	E-Government Act
EO	Executive Order
FFMIA	Federal Financial Management Improvement Act
FS	Food Stamps
GMRA	Government Management Reform Act
GPRA	Government Performance and Results Act
GPRMA	Government Performance and Results Modernization Act
ICMA	International City/County Management Association
IICS	International Index of Citizen Satisfaction
IRS	Internal Revenue Service
IT	information technology
ITA	information technology architecture
MLR	multiple linear regression
NPM	New Public Management
NPS	National Parks Service
NQRC	National Quality Research Center
OMB	Office of Management and Budget
PART	Program Assessment Rating Tool
PBB	performance-based budgeting
PS	Passport Services
RDD	random-digit-dial

SCSB   Swedish Customer Satisfaction Barometer
SEM   structural equation modeling
SSA   Social Security Administration
TSA   Transportation Security Administration
VA   Veterans Affairs
VHA   Veterans Health Administration

Introduction

Overview of the Book

This is a book about a concept, a concept that pervades and influences most aspects of human life: *satisfaction*. We strive to attain satisfaction in our most basic but most important life experiences, including work, health, sex, love, the places we live, the life experiences that define us, the goods and services we consume, and so forth. When satisfied with any and all of these aspects of life, human beings are generally happy and content; when dissatisfied, they are unsettled, unhappy, and prone to seek alternatives. But this book will not attempt to consider the nature of satisfaction with each and every area of human life to which the concept might be applied; after all, the terms "satisfied" and "dissatisfied" might be employed as a means for evaluating virtually every human experience, and this is precisely what makes the concept so powerful. Yet examining satisfaction in such a holistic fashion would be a huge task, one that various others have already (at least in part) attempted. Instead, this is a book about satisfaction with a particular set of experiences endemic to the life of virtually every human being on the planet—satisfaction with government, or what we will call throughout the text, *citizen satisfaction*.

The previous sentence, and the very idea of "satisfied citizens," will likely make some readers cringe. Government is, after all, viewed by many (and especially many contemporary Americans) as nothing more than a burden—and a large, intrinsically dissatisfying burden at that. It takes money from us in the form of taxes, supported by both implicit and explicit threats of punishment for those who refuse to pay, and for many people it is perceived (rightly or wrongly) to provide little in return in the way of high-quality services. What is more, few are convinced that this generally dissatisfying situation can ever truly be rectified or corrected. Government is what it is, things have always been this way, and so long as there is government will always be so. On this view, there are just three universals in the world—death, taxes, and dissatisfying government—with the last two, and maybe all three, going hand-in-hand, of course.

Yet if these all-too-common perceptions of government are justified, then this book is a nonstarter. If government is as universally, inherently and irrevocably dissatisfying as many people believe, and if its prospects for improvement are as bleak as some would suggest, then I should probably save a great deal of time (both yours and mine) and stop writing now. However, as I will argue and explain throughout the chapters that follow, not only is government not necessarily as dissatisfying as many would believe, but it can and has improved (or at least some of its components have improved) in how it interacts with and in what it offers citizens over time. Government *can* be satisfying, I will argue, and it is one of the core purposes of this book to provide evidence of this truth, and to hopefully assist those interested in achieving this goal in some small way—government officials, elected politicians, researchers, and citizens alike.

While it is my hope to make this book accessible to the layperson, it will likely prove most useful and interesting to the student of public administration or public management, the academic researcher, the bureaucratic practitioner and/or researcher, and the policymaker. In the chapters that follow, we will ask and answer a wide variety of questions related to citizen satisfaction. What is citizen satisfaction? How (and why) has citizen satisfaction become an increasingly important topic among those interested in government performance measurement, and especially measurement of administrative (or bureaucratic) institutions? Why should citizen satisfaction be a central concept and a focal point for citizens, academic researchers, students of political science and public administration, and elected officials and other policymakers, both in the United States and in governments around the world? How do you measure the satisfaction of "customers" of government processes and services and utilize this data to improve the delivery of these goods, while at the same time optimally and efficiently allocating scarce and valuable government resources?[1] Perhaps most importantly, given the widespread and growing skepticism among citizens about their own governments, how can improved citizen satisfaction lead to enhanced citizen trust, to a group of citizens more likely to rely on, believe in, and look positively at the institutions and actors exercising power in their society?

And with that, we now begin our journey into citizen satisfaction, starting first with some of the most basic questions, but questions that nonetheless require more complete answers before we proceed: What do we mean by the concept "satisfaction" in general, and by "citizen satisfaction" in particular?

What Is Citizen Satisfaction?

It is often helpful when investigating a rich, complex concept to first spend at least a moment learning about its origins, and even to delve a little deeper and learn how the concept came to "mean what it means" today. Like many commonplace words in the modern English language, the term "satisfaction" is an old one with deep roots in earlier languages. Derived from the Latin words for "enough" (*satis*) and "perform" (*facere*), the word satisfaction in English prior to the sixteenth century had a predominantly religious connotation devoid of its common meaning today. Prior to this time the word in English was almost exclusively associated with Christian theology, and more precisely with the "satisfaction theory of atonement." The satisfaction theory of atonement relates to the suffering of Christ as a substitute for similar suffering among all of humanity, that Christ's sacrifice had "satisfied" the demands of God, or that Christ had "done enough" to assume all of man's sins in the eyes of God. By this usage, "satisfaction" means something closer to "making amends" or "providing adequate restitution" than to *experiencing sufficient gratification and contentment*, as the word is now typically used today.

By the sixteenth century, the meaning of the word in common usage had changed, and had evolved to more closely approximate the concept as it is used today. As seen in the work of the most prominent English author of the time, William Shakespeare, "satisfy" had come to mean *pleasure, happiness or contentment with an experience or outcome*, as portrayed by the heroine Portia in Shakespeare's *The Merchant of Venice*:

> He is well paid that is well satisfied;
> And I, delivering you, am satisfied
> And therein do account myself well paid.[2]

The term satisfaction had at this point evolved to convey something at least much closer to its meaning today: satisfaction as gratification or happiness on the part of the individual with an experience or outcome, conferring the sentiment that an outcome one is focused on and evaluating has provided "enough" (or sufficient) "performance" to realize this gratification and happiness.[3]

But it wasn't until the early twentieth century that the satisfaction concept began to attract greater interest from academics in the social sciences, first in applied psychology and soon thereafter in economics, business, and marketing. Moreover, while still relatively unspecified as a concept and devoid of a technical definition (something academics often enjoy contriving), the word began to appear connected to one of two important nouns: "consumer" or "customer." Indeed, over the first half of the twentieth century, a small but progressively increasing number of references to "consumer satisfaction" as a vital free market business imperative began to appear in all of the psychology, marketing, and economics literatures.[4]

Some of the earliest work on satisfaction was in the field of applied psychology, and in this area studies focused mostly on job or employment satisfaction, and on qualities inside the firm that resulted in this outcome, rather than on the firm's external relationship with its customers. In other works in psychology, satisfying the consumer was referenced as a task central to the firm's sales and advertising missions, thus gradually beginning to focus the concept outside the firm, while related work in marketing and economics at the time began to regard satisfaction as a desirable business outcome overall. While no hard research investigating the concept in expansive detail yet existed, the idea of consumer satisfaction—of making the company's customers happy, contented, and gratified with the products or services being offered—had begun to seep into the business vernacular.

In the mid-1950s, the satisfaction concept would take a major leap forward that would prove vital for its development as a significant object of inquiry in the social sciences, and in particular in understanding human decision-making. In his seminal research in the 1940s and 1950s, economist, political scientist, and (later) Nobel Prize winner Herbert A. Simon introduced the concept of "satisficing," a cognitive-psychological process through which individuals are hypothesized to select an alternative (among any hypothetical set of choices) most likely to result in "satisfaction maximization" with an outcome, given certain limitations to memory, knowledge, and cognitive ability. While Simon was not focused on the individual consumer's satisfaction with a private or public sector consumption experience per se (but rather with how individuals inside organizations made decisions and behave), his work was vital to the development of both rational choice theory and behavioral economics, outlining how when making choices (in virtually any domain of life) individuals tend to be imperfect satisfaction seekers, first and foremost. In turn, these ideas were essential to the business, economics, and marketing disciplines coming to view human beings (and consumers in particular) as rational decision makers out to maximize their own personal contentment with an experience—and to begin to think more seriously about the causes and consequences of consumer satisfaction.[5] And as a result, a more rigorous use of the satisfaction concept would be followed in other disciplines in the subsequent decades, one that would focus more specifically on how and why some experiences tend to result in satisfaction, while others do not.

Thus while the concept of consumer and customer satisfaction appears sporadically in the academic literature in the first half of the twentieth century, and while the idea that decision-making in most areas of human life was critically related to satisfaction maximization in the work of Simon, greatly enhancing serious interest in the concept overall, little rigorous, in-depth analytical work was done on the topic until the 1960s and 1970s, at which time both public administration and marketing scholars began to investigate what precisely it meant to "be satisfied," what *influenced or caused satisfaction and dissatisfaction*, how satisfaction *impacted future behaviors*, the *consequences of satisfaction and its outcomes to organizational performance*, and so forth. It was as a result of these critical "first generation" works that the contemporary focus on satisfaction—again, in both marketing and public administration—emerged.

Today and since the 1960s, insightful and practically applicable work focused on understanding satisfaction (across innumerable contexts) has proliferated. While an exhaustive review of the academic literature on satisfaction across all of the different disciplines where the concept is used from the 1960s to now is unnecessary (a variety of cross-disciplinary references are provided in the bibliography for those interested in beginning a more thorough literature review), suffice it to say that citizen satisfaction in particular is now a highly significant focus among both academics and policymakers. Much of the earliest rigorous work on citizen satisfaction centered around satisfaction with urban or local government services, and more specifically with the provision of urban police services.[6] This strain of citizen satisfaction research remains very much active today, and among both academics and practitioners (including local governments themselves), measuring the satisfaction of citizens with a range of local, municipal, and urban services is quite common.[7]

Furthermore, by the 1990s this literature had moved beyond predominantly studies of local government and began to investigate what influenced satisfaction with the state/regional and federal/national levels of government, and particularly citizen satisfaction with experiences with government bureaucrats and bureaucracies at these levels. And much like the research in other academic areas, the primary goal of this gradually expanding body of research on citizen satisfaction was to discover the factors that made citizens satisfied—or happy, fulfilled, and contented with the performance of government and the outcome of their experiences—and to better understand the consequences of citizen satisfaction and dissatisfaction for these administrative organizations. Studies in this area have examined citizen satisfaction with a range of kinds of federal (or national) government experiences, covering institutions as a whole, specific government services, overall regime performance, and so forth, and have been undertaken both in the United States and in various other nations as well.[8] Importantly and worth noting here, most studies of citizen satisfaction have focused on satisfaction with administrative institutions (i.e., the bureaucracy), rather than with elected officials, other kinds of appointed officials (such as judges), specific laws or policies, and so forth, and in most of what follows in this text we will adopt the same focus. Below and again in chapter 3, we offer additional explanation and justification for this approach to citizen satisfaction measurement.

Yet as we will discuss in some of the chapters that lie ahead (and particularly chapter 1), perhaps the most important recent development in citizen satisfaction research has come not from within the academic literature, but rather from a diffusion of the application of satisfaction research from the private sector to government institutions. Since the early 1990s, inspired by the "reinventing government" movement in the United States and New Public Management (NPM) advocates worldwide, government agencies, outside regulatory agencies, watchdog groups, and a variety of other institutions and officials have become infinitely more interested in measuring and monitoring citizen satisfaction.[9] The goal of this burgeoning governmental practice, as we shall see in what lies ahead, is to use the results of citizen satisfaction measurement to improve citizen perceptions of government performance in a manner similar to the use of consumer satisfaction data in the private sector, and thus to improve the processes, services, products, and so forth, offered to citizens by government.

Therefore, in sum and to tie this brief review of the satisfaction concept and research to what will follow in the text, here we will look at citizen satisfaction as: individual citizens' (in the aggregate) happiness or contentment (or what another author has called the "fulfillment response") with an experience or experiences with the services (or goods, or processes, or programs) provided by government bureaucracies and administrative institutions.[10] The chapters that follow will show how and why this activity has become important (for both researchers and governments themselves), the justifications and purposes for this activity, the statistical methods that can be used for identifying the factors that most strongly drive satisfaction and the vital outcomes of satisfaction, how satisfaction research can help improve government services in a manner most efficient and pleasing to citizens, and why satisfaction research is growing, and is likely to grow even more vital in the future. This, then, is what we define citizen satisfaction to be, and how we will approach our work in elucidating the concept in the chapters that follow.

Two final caveats before we proceed. As mentioned briefly above, and as we will remind the reader at various points throughout the text, we will focus specifically and almost exclusively on citizen satisfaction with *US federal* government *bureaucracies or administrative institutions* in this book, while eschewing examination of citizen satisfaction with other levels of government and other aspects of the political system to which it might be applied, such as political parties, elected officials, politically generated public policy, and so forth. On the one hand, we focus here on national/federal level institutions precisely because substantially less literature and research in this area exists (and on the United States in particular because of the availability of data). As the list of references below will reveal, the quantity and longevity of studies into citizen satisfaction at the local government level makes additional research in this area somewhat less important, in our opinion.

On the other hand, the focus here on bureaucratic or administration institutions is due to the particular importance of this kind of research for improving these bureaucracies' processes, products and services in a manner that better satisfies citizens, as we will evidence in several of the chapters that follow. Unlike the political system in democracies the world over, bureaucratic institutions simply have a greater need for this kind of research, as they lack the feedback mechanisms enjoyed by democratic polities provided through elections. However, perhaps even more important than these considerations is the fact that citizen satisfaction research ought to be, in our estimation, an apolitical activity, one that *should be lauded and advocated regardless of political inclination.* Whether "bigger" or "smaller" government is one's preference, it seems fair to say that all citizens would prefer that the services offered by government be provided in a better, more satisfying manner. So for this reason, we will pursue our project in this text while avoiding politicization of the topic to as great an extent possible.

While we will leave this brief conceptual and literature review and statement of purpose for now, in the chapters that follow much of this research—as well as a host of additional works—will be referenced and discussed vis-a-vis the theory and practice of citizen satisfaction measurement.

The American Customer Satisfaction Index

A considerable portion of the research, data, practical insights, and experiences that guide and inform the material in this book come from the author's experience working as the Director of Research at the American Customer Satisfaction Index (ACSI) over the past decade. For this reason alone, a brief introduction to the ACSI is warranted before proceeding. But because ACSI has been and remains a valuable resource for both public and private sector satisfaction data, and a wealth of research of all kinds utilizing and relying on this data, this introduction may be useful for several additional reasons.

The ACSI was founded in Ann Arbor, Michigan by a research group within the University of Michigan's business school called the National Quality Research Center (NQRC). The NQRC and ACSI were the brain children of Professor Claes Fornell. A native of Sweden, in 1989 Fornell started, with support from the Swedish government, a national index of customer satisfaction called the Swedish Customer Satisfaction Barometer (SCSB). It was the SCSB model for measuring satisfaction—the first such research project to apply a standardized model for measuring satisfaction across the entirety of an economy's diverse industries and sectors—that Fornell transported across the Atlantic and applied to the much larger US economy. With the support of several prominent business professors and researchers at UM's School of Business (now the Stephen M. Ross School of Business), and with financial assistance from both the university and the American Society for Quality (ASQ) in Milwaukee, Wisconsin, Fornell launched the ACSI in the fall of 1994.

The core idea motivating Fornell to create both the SCSB and the ACSI was simple. While governments and researchers had long measured the quantity of economic output produced within national economies through a range of diverse metrics, they had largely ignored a more elusive feature of these economies that was as important if not more so—the *quality* of economic output. While metrics of total economic production were typically viewed as vital tools for judging and forecasting economic success, Fornell recognized that growing competition (both domestic and international competition) and increased consumer choice (and power) demanded a better understanding of what motivated consumers to open their wallets and spend their hard-earned dollars on some goods and services rather than others. Measuring satisfaction in a systematic, scientific manner would therefore provide the missing piece in fully understanding the health of companies and entire national economies from the perspective of the ultimate and most important judge, the consumer.

While therefore focused on measuring consumer satisfaction with private sector goods and services in the beginning, the research team behind ACSI recognized that the sheer size and economic importance of government in the United States necessitated measuring the satisfaction of the consumers of these organizations as well. Government was simply too large and vital a part of almost every economy to be ignored, and in some nations makes up a significant part (and even a majority) of total economic output (i.e., gross domestic product). These facts, along with the early influence of Barbara Everitt Bryant, the managing director of ACSI at its inception and a former director of the Census under President George H. W. Bush, ACSI researchers decided to measure satisfaction with government services as well. As such, beginning in 1994 with its pilot project, ACSI included both core local government (police and waste disposal) and some federal government (the IRS) services for annual measurement.

In 1999, ACSI's measurement of government services—and in particular, federal government services—expanded significantly. In that year, the Office of Management and Budget (OMB) under the administration of President Bill Clinton—an administration that prided itself on its efforts to reform, streamline, and improve the bureaucratic system—selected the ACSI as the "gold standard" measure of citizen satisfaction for the US federal government, resulting in a large, administration-funded, cross-departmental satisfaction measurement project including most of the highest-profile federal agencies. And since 1999, the ACSI's measurement of government at all levels has expanded considerably. Variants of this model have been used to measure satisfaction with literally hundreds of government programs, agencies, and departments, as well as a huge number of e-government websites and other government contact points. Furthermore, ACSI's methods and models are used to measure satisfaction with government services across all levels of government, including local, state, and federal government. Finally, as part of an effort to "export" the ACSI project to other countries via partnerships with research groups in those countries, the ACSI methodology and model is now being deployed in more than a dozen nations outside the United States, and this includes government measurement in most of these countries.

This brief history of the ACSI project was necessary, as mentioned above, to both provide background for much of the research and experience that guides the author's expertise in writing on this particular topic—citizen satisfaction—while also serving as an important introduction to the source of much of the data that the book relies upon. Today the ACSI project remains a useful source for satisfaction data for both the private and public sectors. In each of the chapters that lie ahead, at least some of this data will help guide the ideas, methods, conclusions, and so forth, that will (we hope) help the reader better understand the nature of citizen satisfaction, its purposes, its measurement, and its value.[11]

Chapter Outline

The remaining chapters in this book are organized as follows. Chapter 1 examines the evolution of government performance measurement over the last few decades, focusing on a brief review of various initiatives (i.e., laws, executive orders, regulations, etc.) in the United States (focusing mostly at the federal level of government) that have mandated various types of measurement. This review of the growth and evolution of government performance measurement is intended to illustrate, among other developments, how governments have begun to shift focus from predominantly internal measures of performance to external, citizen-centric approaches. In turn, these external metrics have dramatically elevated the importance of measuring the perspective of the actual users, consumers and citizens experiencing the services to performance measurement in general, with citizen satisfaction measurement arising as the most visible of these citizen-centric approaches. The chapter concludes by arguing that this evolution towards citizen-centered performance measures should continue and even advance further, much like they have in the private sector.

Following from this, chapter 2 offers a detailed discussion of many of the purposes of and justifications for undertaking citizen satisfaction measurement. This chapter describes several of the most common objectives underpinning this practice vis-a-vis administrative or bureaucratic institutions, along with a variety of important internal and external purposes the data can serve. Included in this list of purposes are the development of a more dynamic feedback loop connecting government and the people they serve, increased government transparency (or openness), enhanced top-down and bottom-up accountability, the rebuilding of trust between citizens and government, effective and efficient process and service quality improvements, the facilitation of benchmarking (or comparison) across units of government towards identifying best practices potentially useful for satisfaction improvement, more efficient budgetary and resource allocation, and as a tool for monitoring and motivating public employees. In sum, chapter 2 answers the "why" question, laying out a host of reasons supporting the measurement of citizen satisfaction.

In chapter 3, we turn from preliminary investigations of citizen satisfaction to the practice of its measurement, focusing on the "how" question (or more accurately, questions), and examining some key methods entailed in citizen satisfaction research, an activity that carries over into chapters 4 and 5 as well. Most importantly, chapter 3 provides a step-by-step review of many of the core issues that must be addressed when first beginning a citizen satisfaction measurement project. Predominantly nontechnical in nature (at least to the extent this is possible), the discussion offers a look at the major phases of the satisfaction measurement process, including the selection of the level or institution of government to measure, identification of the population or segment of citizen-customers—and the corresponding government agency or program—to measure, selection of key factors that drive citizen satisfaction and factors that are influenced by satisfaction prior to questionnaire creation, conceptualization of the satisfaction concept itself, development of the survey questionnaire, and the collection of data.

In chapter 4, a review of some statistical methods that can be (and often are) used to examine the data collected from a satisfaction survey instrument (or questionnaire) is provided. While there are many, many extant statistical methods available for examining all different kinds of survey data, chapter 4 suggests that one type of statistical analysis—a multivariate (latent variable) structural equation modeling approach—provides an optimal and well-tested technique for both generating valid, reliable satisfaction scores and for relating satisfaction to its key drivers (or influencing factors) and outcomes (or consequences). In turn, or so we will suggest, this kind of data analysis can offer the most useful, accurate, and actionable insights into the practical reforms government agencies can make toward improving citizen satisfaction, as well as related outcomes like citizen trust. While somewhat more technical than the other chapters by necessity, it should nonetheless provide the reader with the benefits and drawbacks of competing statistical techniques that may be considered when analyzing satisfaction data.

Following this, chapter 5 provides an examination of the practical use of satisfaction data for drawing conclusions and making decisions aimed at improving citizen perceptions with government. First, techniques for using the "priority matrix" tool to identify the most important areas in need of improvement toward increased satisfaction are discussed. Next, a method for the centralized, government-wide prioritization of performance improvements based on analyses of performance data is developed. Using a multiyear sample of citizen satisfaction data from the US federal government, some of the same data already reviewed in earlier chapters, we examine how this data, along with relatively little additional external information, can guide reform priorities from the highest (departmental) levels down to the agency, program and individual government program levels. The ultimate aim of the "multidimensional" approach we outline in this chapter is to optimize the services delivered to citizens to achieve maximum effect in improving citizen satisfaction and citizen trust throughout the government, both vertically and horizontally.

In chapter 6, an investigation of some general but nonetheless vital findings gleaned from historical citizen satisfaction data is provided. Examining a large sample of data collected and analyzed over nearly two decades by the ACSI, the primary goal of chapter 6 is to consider some enduring lessons about citizen satisfaction performance, and to show these findings both over time and in relation to comparable private sector data (where applicable). Some of the key findings discussed in the chapter include comparisons of public and private sector satisfaction, the ability of some units of government to meet (and even exceed) comparable private sector experiences, the role of citizens' depressed expectations in dampening their satisfaction, and the relationship between satisfaction and trust in government, along with other topics.

Finally, in chapter 7 we expand our view and discuss the use of citizen satisfaction and performance measurement data as a vital resource for the international community for both benchmarking and improving government performance around the world. We begin by reviewing the pressures likely to impact governments across the globe over the next century, where growing and "graying" populations, along with already-ballooning government debt, are likely to force most governments to serve more citizens with fewer resources. We then provide an outline or framework for cross-national citizen satisfaction measurement of government services, and advocate an "International Citizen Satisfaction Index." If designed correctly, such a system could provide, we argue, a standard of high-quality, satisfying government capable of serving as a benchmarking tool and source of intergovernmental knowledge exchange for governments around the world. In turn, this tool could provide valuable insights to governments struggling to maintain services for more demanding, fast-growing populations, and to provide satisfying government that enhances citizen trust under stressful conditions.

CHAPTER 1

Government Performance Measurement Comes of Age

Introduction

Government performance measurement is not a new phenomenon. Basic measures of government performance have existed for decades, and some for even longer. Nevertheless, over the last 20 years or so governments at all levels have become almost fixated on systematic and scientific measures of performance. The inspiration for this focus has come in part from the private sector. Like many private sector firms, a majority of which now routinely dissect nearly every aspect of their company's production processes, supply chain, service quality, customer relationships, customer satisfaction, and so forth, through oftentimes complex systems of performance measurement, governments have followed suit and devised innumerable methods for measuring, monitoring, and benchmarking the performance of their various programs, agencies, and departments.

In this chapter, we begin by providing a brief definition of performance measurement, and then examine the evolution of government performance measurement over the last few decades. Here we focus on a review of key laws, regulations, and initiatives that have mandated various types of performance measurement. While we focus on the federal level of government in the United States, mostly due to the huge diversity of these initiatives at other levels of government and across national boundaries, many of these same kinds of initiatives—and the general pattern of performance measurement adoption and evolution we will outline here—is certainly not unique to the US federal government. Indeed, systems of performance measurement have emerged from among governments at all levels, and in governments around the world. Nevertheless, our review focuses on a look at legislation from the US Congress, as well as some presidential initiatives and executive orders enacted predominantly since the early 1990s.

Our review of the growth and evolution of government performance measurement reveals that, in a pattern similar to what has occurred in the private sector, and in part precisely because of this private sector evolution and its influence on the public sector, governments have begun to shift their focus from predominantly internal measures of performance to external, citizen-centered measures. That is, instead of focusing (almost exclusively) on internal evaluations of unit or agency performance conducted by actors within the institutions being evaluated (or related oversight agencies) and governed by internal criteria of performance success, these external measures highlight the importance of the perspective of the users, consumers, and citizens experiencing the services delivered by government.

The chapter concludes by arguing that the evolution toward external, citizen-centered performance measures likely will—and absolutely should—continue. Through an argument linking the dramatic growth in consumer power in the free market (due in large part to the growth in information accessibility realized through the Information Age) and citizen power (in democratic and nondemocratic societies alike), we suggest that external, citizen-centric performance measures are essential today.

A Review of Performance Management and Measurement Legislation in the United States

Attempts to reform the management practices of the US federal government are almost as old as the government itself. Efforts to achieve this goal through systems of performance measurement, while not quite as old, are nearly so. In its most basic form, performance measurement entails nothing more than the "regular measurement of the results (outcomes) and efficiency of [government] services or programs," and since these kinds of metrics can come in a diverse array of shapes and sizes, governments have in fact long undertaken performance measurement initiatives, though some more complex and sophisticated than others.[1] In essence, performance measurement is conducted anytime an organization attempts to systematically gauge and quantify its success in achieving some fundamental goal, objective, or mission, and thus performance measurement is certainly not a new phenomenon.

Yet over the last few decades the quantity, the complexity, the rigor, and the focus of these performance measurement efforts have all changed.[2] A brief review of some of the recent and most important initiatives aimed at realizing improvement through performance measurement should make both the increase in intensity and the shift in focus apparent. For simplicity's sake, we offer a short synopsis of each initiative (or law, executive order, etc.), followed by a summary of the primary performance measurement objective pursued in the initiative. And as mentioned earlier, this brief review will set the stage for an essential point we elaborate on later: Performance measurement initiatives have increasingly shifted from a focus on internal, agency-based analysis to external, citizen-centered analysis.

Chief Financial Officers Act of 1990

Passed by Congress in 1990 and signed into law by President George H. W. Bush, the *Chief Financial Officers (CFO) Act of 1990* sought to standardize and better regulate the budgeting and accounting practices of the federal government. Among its features, the CFO Act mandated a single chief financial officer for each applicable federal agency, thus better imitating the model of financial management found in the private sector. The CFO Act further aimed to centralize and make more transparent the accounting practices of federal agencies by empowering a government-wide chief financial officer, the Deputy Director for Management, within the Office of Management and Budget (OMB), a single individual responsible for monitoring the accounting practices of all agencies.

Performance Measurement Objective: The changes introduced by the CFO Act were intended to improve federal agency financial management by centralizing these practices, while also providing key budgetary information (i.e., performance data) to a single, centralized chief financial officer capable of making cross-agency performance comparisons (i.e., benchmarking).

Government Performance and Results Act of 1993

The *Government Performance and Results Act (GPRA) of 1993* was considered a major innovation in federal government performance measurement at the time of its passage, and the legislation remains highly influential today (see below). A product of the "reinventing government" movement dominant in the late 1980s and early 1990s, and the related government-wide "National Performance Review" directed by Vice President Al Gore in 1993, the GPRA mandated that all applicable federal agencies and departments create annual strategic plans, review performance relative to these plans, and produce annual "performance reports." Prepared for submission to Congress and the OMB, these reports were intended to outline areas of both performance success and failure, detail actions the agency planned to implement toward improving areas found to be deficient, and to recommend future adjustments in performance goals.

Performance Measurement Objective: While the GPRA was diverse in its focus and the types of performance metrics mandated, a central goal of the legislation was to increase public confidence in the federal government through a renewed (or new) emphasis on performance measurement aimed at improved program efficiency and higher quality services delivered to citizens. A portion of the latter was to come directly via citizen-customer feedback and surveys, the first such government-wide mandate by the federal government.

Government Management Reform Act of 1994 and the Federal Financial Management Improvement Act of 1996

While primarily an addendum to provisions included in the CFO Act of 1990, the *Government Management Reform Act (GMRA) of 1994* attempted to further modernize the accounting practices of federal agencies and bring them even more into line with private sector practices. The GMRA mandated independent, audited financial statements of all applicable federal agencies and departments, primarily as a means of better tracking and managing the financial performance of these agencies. The *Federal Financial Management Improvement Act (FFMIA) of 1996* would advance this agenda a step further, creating federal agency-wide accounting standards and external checks on compliance with these standards.

Performance Measurement Objective: Much like the CFO Act of 1990 before it, the GMRA and the FFMIA aimed at improved federal government performance through the adoption of new budgetary management techniques, and improved budgeting and accounting performance measurement.

Information Technology Management Reform Act of 1996

The *Information Technology Management Reform Act of 1996*, sometimes also called the Clinger-Cohen Act (after its Congressional authors), sought to reduce waste—in the form of excess bureaucratic paperwork—and streamline myriad federal government processes through the adoption of information technologies (IT) already commonplace in the private sector. Like the CFO Act of 1990 and the GMRA of 1994, the Clinger-Cohen Act aimed to achieve these goals in part through the reform of management practices, with each agency thereafter required to create the position of chief information officer, who would in turn outline and implement an integrated "information technology architecture" (ITA). Clinger-Cohen also aimed to measure the performance of these newly mandated IT systems from the perspective of reduced waste and reduced expenditure, while also requiring extensive performance measurement of these new IT systems for the purposes of interagency benchmarking of process quality, and the quality of outputs and outcomes.

Performance Measurement Objective: While Clinger-Cohen is often credited first and foremost with ushering in the era of electronic government (or "e-government") in the United States, it also exemplifies the heightened focus on performance measurement emerging in the federal government during this period, as these new IT systems were from the start to be rigorously monitored and measured for their performance success and accomplishment of core goals and objectives.

The Program Assessment Rating Tool

Enacted in 2002 by the "President's Management Council" within the OMB, the Program Assessment Rating Tool (PART) was the most significant performance measurement and management initiative enacted during the administration of President George W. Bush.

The PART was explicitly designed to better achieve the core performance measurement mission of the GPRA legislation enacted almost a decade earlier, and to do so through a four-category rating system applied to nearly every federal agency centered on the agency's program design, strategic planning, program management, and program results. Going beyond GPRA and other earlier initiatives, the PART was also intended to provide a means for undertaking "performance-based budgeting," where agency and program funding decisions (and even the continued existence of some programs) were to be determined in part by their success on a set of unified cross-agency performance standards. Because it demanded the use of common metrics for gauging performance, the PART also facilitated means for effectively and accurately benchmarking performance across all of the measured agencies.

Performance Measurement Objective: The PART represented a first attempt by the federal government to provide a systematic, unified, and government-wide performance measurement system encompassing a variety of types of metrics, including internal assessment of agency performance, external assessment (through customer feedback), and more efficient budgetary resource allocation through performance-based budgeting.

E-Government Act of 2002

Passed in 2002, the *E-Government Act (EGA)* was a statute aimed at advancing the e-government capabilities of the federal government as a whole. While most federal agencies had by this time already introduced e-government tools for providing services to citizens (and were required to do so by the aforementioned Clinger-Cohen Act), the EGA was created with the recognition that federal government had not yet done so at a level consistent with the best practices of the private sector. The EGA thus mandated centralized leadership, through a new government-wide chief information officer and a new "Office of Electronic Government," as well as some central government funding, aimed at creating a comprehensive and unified electronic infrastructure capable of integrating information technology (and especially a system of modern, high-functioning agency websites) into essentially all of the activities of the federal government.

Performance Measurement Objective: While the EGA aimed primarily at improving agency performance through the adoption of more and better e-government resources, it also sought to achieve this goal through a range of new performance metrics, including explicit demands that performance measures of the impact of e-government on customer service delivery be devised.

Executive Order 13450

Executive Order (EO) 13450 was signed by President George W. Bush in late 2007. Primarily an attempt to formalize the system of performance measurement enacted through the PART, EO 13450 does so in a unique way, by mandating the creation of the position of "Program Improvement Officer" within each applicable agency. EO 13450 also created the "Performance Improvement Council" within OMB, a group tasked with monitoring program performance and performance measurement government-wide. Finally, EO 13450 requires each agency to publish the results of its latest performance review on its agency website for public review, increasing public transparency of the performance measurement process.

Performance Measurement Objective: The main goal of EO 13450 was to formalize the type of performance measurement—and, it was hoped, to permanently institute it after George W. Bush's second term had ended—advocated by the PART, while also demanding greater transparency in the delivery of performance information.

Government Performance and Results Modernization Act of 2010

The *Government Performance and Results Modernization Act (GPRMA) of 2010* represents the first substantial legislative revision to the GPRA of 1993. Building on the GPRA, the GPRMA codified into law several aspects of EO 13450 (discussed above), including the designation of Performance Improvement Officers within agencies and the Performance Improvement Council within OMB. GPMRA also requires agencies to submit their performance plans and regular performance reviews through a new government website designed for this purpose, instead of submitting them independently each year to Congress.

Performance Measurement Objective: While mostly an update of the GPRA with the added benefit of two decades of experience implementing that legislation, the GPMRA demands greater centralized control over performance measurement, as well as greater public transparency of performance plans and performance measurement results.

H. R. 1660, Government Customer Service Improvement Act of 2013

At the time of this writing, House Resolution (H. R.) 1660 (also called the "Government Customer Service Improvement Act") had just been passed through the House of Representatives, but had not yet been passed by the Senate or signed into law. While it may still never become law, it has bipartisan support and seems likely headed to final approval. Regardless of its ultimate fate, this resolution provides important insight into the latest thinking vis-à-vis performance measurement, management, and improvement within the US federal government. In sum, H. R. 1660 advocates the creation of a single, unified set of customer service quality standards for federal government agencies, including the creation of a standardized set of response times for email, telephone calls, processing of applications, and so forth. Agency performance under these new unified standards is from the beginning to be measured and monitored through a new "customer service feedback system to collect information from customers of the agency"—by surveying citizen-customers about their experiences with agencies and those agency's performance.

Performance Measurement Objective: Unlike all of the earlier legislation and initiatives outlined above, including the GPRA and the Bush administration's PART initiative, H. R. 1660 focuses almost exclusively on performance measurement aimed at service quality improvements, improvements to be monitored largely through customer feedback and surveying (see table 1.1).

This brief review of the recent history of performance measurement initiatives within the US federal government reveals several things. In the first instance, it illustrates the intensified focus on performance measurement over the past 20 years in the United States. While we do not have the space to undertake a comprehensive review

Table 1.1 A summary of recent performance measurement initiatives in the United States

Initiative	Summary
Chief Financial Officers Act of 1990	Improve federal agency financial management through centralization and budgetary performance data
Government Performance and Results Act of 1993	Mandates myriad systematized performance metrics, both internal and external
Government Management Reform Act of 1994 and the Federal Financial Management Improvement Act of 1996	Adoption of new budgetary management techniques and improved budgeting and accounting performance measurement
Information Technology Management Reform Act of 1996	Adoption and measurement of new IT systems in government
The Program Assessment Rating Tool	A government-wide performance measurement system, including internal assessment, external assessment (through customer feedback), and performance-based budgeting
E-Government Act of 2002	Performance measurement of the impact of federal e-government on customer service delivery
Executive Order 13450	Formalize and standardize the practices of the Program Assessment Rating Tool
Government Performance and Results Modernization Act of 2010	Update to the Government Performance and Results Act of 1993
House Resolution 1660	Performance measurement aimed at service quality improvements through customer feedback surveys

back to 1791,[3] few would deny that the US federal government (and a vast majority of governments elsewhere) has grown decidedly more interested in performance measurement during this period that at any time previously.[4] Moreover, this intensified interest in performance measurement has been diverse and multifaceted, aimed at the improved measurement of accounting standards and practices, robust measurement and monitoring of newly implemented systems (such as IT systems), true and effective performance-based budgeting, and the analysis of citizen-customer feedback gleaned through surveying actual citizen-users of these agencies. Furthermore, this review shows that the focus on performance measurement has stretched across political ideologies, as left- and right-leaning presidential administrations alike have taken up the banner. Perhaps most importantly, though, has been the gradual shift toward external, citizen-centered performance measurement that, we will argue, is visible in the historical trajectory of the initiatives outlined above. Given the importance of this shift, it deserves more detailed attention.

Consumer Power and Citizen-Centered Performance Measurement

Before we proceed to discuss the shift in focus from internal to external or citizen-centered types of performance measurement that we argue the review undertaken above helps reveal, it is important that we first pause and outline precisely what we mean by these two varieties of measurement. Indeed, a fuller understanding of these two perspectives should help clarify the shift in focus as it has occurred within the US federal government. This discussion will also put us in a better position to both support this shift, and to argue for its continued development and advancement in the future.

Internal versus External Performance Measurement

Like most phenomena of this kind, organizational performance measurement (including its implementation in both the public and the private sectors) can and has taken a variety of forms. While stark definitions might make things easier to understand, performance measurement is simply not an undifferentiated, one-dimensional activity that means the same thing to all those involved. Yet in relation to the varieties of performance metrics most regularly adopted by governments, two general perspectives on how to conduct this measurement to optimal effect have tended to dominate, and effectively encompass most kinds of such measurement: internal and external performance measurement.[5] We begin by discussing internal metrics.

Internal measures of performance are labeled such because of both who defines the criteria of success and who is responsible for measuring achievement of these criteria. That is, internal performance measures are derived from an ideal of "successful performance" defined and measured by administrators, researchers, experts or other personnel *internal to the organization* (or agency, or program, etc.) being examined, and these measures rely first and foremost on criteria of performance and internal actors (those professionals working within an organization measuring its performance) to evaluate success. A few examples of internal performance metrics, taken from both the private and public sectors, may help clarify this type.

In the private sector, internal performance metrics can and do take a wide variety of forms, and include activities that standardize and measure internal processes (such as production efficiency, service delivery times, and so forth), as well as the full range of financial performance metrics most companies monitor, including market share, revenue growth, earnings-per-share, and so on. In the public sector, internal performance metrics are similar, but are (obviously) adjusted for the unique nature and purpose of public sectors organizations. These government-specific internal performance metrics can range from simple comparisons between the projected and actual accomplishment of some broad organizational mission (for instance, "has program X met its goal of reducing poverty, increasing literacy, or combating cancer?"), to internally verifiable evaluations of finite aspects of service delivery relative to established goals (for instance, an agency setting a goal of 30 days for processing applications, or 48 hours for responding to a citizen's request, and comparing average actual delivery time with this goal). Yet these are only truly "internal" measures if they rely on bureaucrats—and in some instances, related but distinct oversight institutions and actors also employed within government, such as the OMB or Congressional committee members and oversight bodies—to set criteria and evaluate performance relative to the criteria.

One popular type of internal performance measure is performance-based budgeting (PBB).[6] Through PBB, program effectiveness is rated relative to budget allocation, and the core performance metric is the program's quantifiable outcome relative to dollars spent. Often within PBB, the size of future budget allocations may be driven by a determination of successful performance relative to past program expenditures. To refer back to the performance measurement legislation and initiatives discussed earlier, the CFO, GMRA, and FFMIA are all fairly clear instances of internal performance measurement, as they rely on internal actors to use internal performance data (in this case, budgetary data) to measure, monitor and compare agency performance. Furthermore, the PART also seeks to take myriad performance measures into account toward making PBB recommendations.

On the other hand, as opposed to a focus on strictly internal criteria and internal actors to judge performance, external performance measurement (which we will also call "citizen-centered" performance measurement at times, for reasons that should become clear) focuses on clients, citizens, users or other stakeholders *external to an organization*—but familiar with and directly impacted by the organization's performance nonetheless—as the means of gauging success. That is, external measures of performance diverge from internal measures both in who evaluates organizational success and in the criteria used to evaluate success.

In both the public and the private sectors, external performance measures typically ask relevant external groups, such as citizens or customers, and almost always through some form of *customer survey* of the individuals within these populations, to evaluate program activities central to the services they have experienced, such as perceptions of customer service delivery, perceptions of the ease or efficiency of application processes, the courteousness of customer service personnel, the accessibility of information disseminated, and so forth.[7] Because the respondents surveyed will usually have had direct experience with the organization under investigation, they are able to provide perceptions based on their own experiences that can prove highly useful to organizations attempting to improve their processes, their service offerings, the performance of their personnel, and so forth.

Again referring back to the performance measurement legislation and initiatives discussed above, several of these can be seen to focus on or at least contain elements of external performance measurement. For instance, portions of the GPRA, and especially those that emphasize citizen satisfaction measurement, illustrate one prominent kind of external performance measurement. Moreover, the PART, the GPRMA, and HR 1660 all focus strongly on external performance measurement, given the considerable attention paid to seeking consumer feedback for measuring and improving agency performance.[8]

The Shift from Internal to External Measures

With these definitions of internal and external performance measurement now at our disposal, the trend toward external measurement over the last decade—at least at the federal level of government in the United States, but a trend that is apparent elsewhere as well—should be clearer. Indeed, our earlier review of the key performance measurement initiatives and legislation shows this shift from predominantly internal to, at the very least, a noticeable increase in focus on citizen-centered measures of performance, and in nearly chronological order. With the important exception of the GPRA of 1993 (and to a lesser extent, the Clinger-Cohen Act), a majority of the central performance measurement initiatives of the 1990s (and earlier) focused almost entirely on internal measurement, and more precisely, centralized internal measurement and management of agency budgetary performance. During this period, organizational management reform was indeed linked to performance measurement, but these measures were to be undertaken first and foremost by actors within government and somewhat narrowly focused on finance and budgeting.

Yet by the early 2000s, starting with the EGA and PART and culminating in the GPRMA and HR 1660, a far greater emphasis has been placed on measurement of performance through the gathering of citizen feedback and related external metrics. Indeed, all of these initiatives place considerable importance on measuring citizen-user perceptions of agencies and their services, with some (such as HR 1660) making external performance measurement the central, fundamental objective. Coinciding with a dramatic increase in attention to "customer service excellence" in government (the roots of which we touch on below), external performance measurement has now clearly come to the forefront, or at minimum gained a place of prominence alongside traditional internal measures.[9]

But the shift from internal to external performance measurement, as we have described it here, raises some questions. Why has this change taken place? Is this change a positive or a negative development? Will this change persist, or will internal measures again overwhelm (or entirely replace) external ones? Beginning with a review of some relevant and related developments in the private sector, we will attempt to answer these questions.

Long Live Citizen-Centered Performance Measurement!

In the private sector, consumers have grown more powerful vis-à-vis sellers or suppliers (i.e., businesses and corporations) than ever before. This newfound and significant growth in "consumer sovereignty," as it is sometimes called, has emerged over just the last 10–15 years. These facts are disputed by almost no one, and there is an equally undeniable explanation for this dramatic growth in consumer power: The development of the Internet and the rise of the Information Age.[10] In turn, as the growth in consumer power has become recognized reality and infiltrated the consciousness of business executives, it has yielded significant changes both in how businesses operate and in how they measure the performance of their operations. No longer are consumers viewed as passive recipients of the goods and services suppliers choose to mass produce and provide; they have become more active, more influential, and therefore more important, and because of this their opinions and perceptions demand (and are receiving from companies) greater attention than ever before.[11] And as we will argue below, these changes have had a similar impact on government and similar consequences for how governments view their interactions with citizens.

But how have the Internet and the dawn of the Information Age made consumers more powerful? To be sure, the ways in which the Information Age—and particularly the mass dissemination of information through the Internet and its easily accessible websites—has empowered consumers are myriad. For the sake of brevity, let's consider just a few of the more obvious (but essential) ways that consumers have gained leverage and power in relation to the companies that sell them good and services:

1. *Greater access to information about specific products and services*: No longer must consumers rely as heavily on the "signals" sent by suppliers—through advertising and related marketing efforts—about product and service offerings, as they can now much more easily conduct independent research about them before purchasing, thereby making more informed consumption choices;

2. *Greater access to information about alternative suppliers*: For much of the era of the "old," pre-Information Age economy, buyers had a limited ability to seek out alternative suppliers for many of the goods and services they needed or wanted. Now, consumers can much more easily identify a nearly unlimited

number of such suppliers, compare features and pricing, and select a company that best suits their needs;

3. *Increased ability of consumers to punish sellers through complaint behavior and word-of-mouth*: One of the primary uses of the Internet is as a vehicle for information exchange both between consumers, and between consumers and the companies they purchase from. Literally millions of blogs and related websites now exist for the sole purpose of this type of exchange. These resources have allowed consumers to more easily relay their grievances with suppliers to both the companies themselves and to other consumers, and to do so across great distances and to much larger audiences;

4. *Increased ability to influence product/service offerings*: Related to the benefits of information exchange via the Internet is the ability of consumers to directly and indirectly influence the goods and services offered by suppliers, either through direct contact with the company or through indirect influence. Through the new networks of communication connecting consumers to their companies introduced via the Internet, and the more rapid changes they can pressure companies to make through this interaction, consumers can now demand "mass customized" goods and services that better meet their individual needs (officially ending the Henry Ford-era of mass standardization).[12]

In these ways, among a host of others, the Information Age has "changed the game" in how buyers and sellers relate to one another, and in the amount of power held by consumers. The changes in business practices resulting from this shift are too numerous to mention here. Yet most important for our purposes, these changes have influenced how private sector firms measure and manage their performance. Whereas companies—and indeed, national economies in their entirety—once relied almost exclusively on measures like labor productivity, gross domestic product, international trade, revenue growth, quarterly profitability, stock market performance, and so forth, as indicators of "success," now external measures (for instance, customer satisfaction, customer loyalty, and word-of-mouth) and the linkages between these measures and financial performance have become far more prominent.[13] Indeed, practices like customer relationship management and customer asset management, and concepts like "customer equity value," "customer-centricity," and "intangible assets" now occupy a central place in the discourse of corporate performance precisely because of this changed landscape.[14]

While these changes have been particularly prominent and noticeable in the private sector, many of the same factors leading to an increase in private sector consumer power have similarly impacted governments, both directly via the changes emerging through the Internet, and indirectly through the influence of the private sector in setting the agenda for government management reform. Regarding the former, all of the above-mentioned sources of consumer power vis-à-vis corporations apply in similar (though not necessarily identical) ways to the public sector. Certainly, the Information Age has created opportunities for citizens to achieve more equal information access vis-à-vis their governments, provided easier access to information about alternative "suppliers" of services (in this case, the services provided by other governments, something we illustrate clearly in chapter 7), along with greater opportunities to both publicly relay grievances and press for government services better matching individual needs. As such, whether they like it or not, governments the world over are confronted with a citizenry that is better informed, more capable of making comparative judgments about alternative "suppliers" of services, and better able to air grievances and demand change. In short, if private sector consumers have realized increased sovereignty as a result of the Information Age, as is often suggested, so too has citizen sovereignty advanced.

What is more, the private sector has exercised enormous influence over both the management and the measurement practices of government over the past two decades, and arguably, the influence of the private on the public sector has never been so great.[15] More specifically, private sector–inspired movements like the Reinventing Government and New Public Management (NPM) movements have guided recent advocates of public sector reform. In general, these movements and their proponents have emphasized types of government agency management modeled after the private sector, a government-wide orientation to high-quality customer service delivery, and the adoption of performance goals and mandatory performance measurement systems mirroring those used in the private sector.

Indeed, the influence of the private sector in guiding reforms to government practice is highlighted in several of the initiatives discussed earlier (in how government has sought to budget like the private sector, create IT offerings guided by private sector best practices, and so on). And given that the private sector has itself shifted focus from internal toward external measures of performance, it stands to reason that the pressures being placed on government from the private sector through these movements have increasingly emphasized external performance measures as well, and will continue to do so.

Given both the realities of the Information Age and the influence the private sector exercises over the public sector, it is likely that governments will continue to pursue external, citizen-centric forms of performance measurement, at least for the foreseeable future. This is not to say that these measures will (nor should) entirely supplant internal measures, which will always have a place in the performance measurement universe. But certainly, it seems clear that this type of external measurement is here to stay, and will only grow in prominence in the years ahead.

Moreover, or so we would argue, the change toward external measures is a positive development that governments should continue to pursue. Much like in the private sector, the new focus on external performance metrics is, in fact, an explicit acceptance that much like private sector consumers, citizens are now more powerful than ever before, that they have more leverage vis-à-vis their governments than ever before, and that they therefore need to be listened to. In a sense, the Information Age has advanced the democratic agenda, in that the recognition of enhanced citizen sovereignty fits well with the democratic ethos pervading many governments in power today.[16] Indeed, eminently democratic values like transparency, accountability, and citizen trust can all be advanced by external performance metrics, and for these reasons, citizen-centric performance measurement carries added value above and beyond its more straightforward purposes.

In the next chapter, we elaborate on many of these justifications for focusing on external performance measurement as they relate to democratic (and other) values, through a discussion of the purposes and objectives of citizen satisfaction measurement. Citizen satisfaction measurement holds, or so we will suggest, enormous potential to both help governments understand the changed landscape of modern, Information Age societies, and to recognize and accept the increased power (and ability to affect change) of the citizens living in this age.

Conclusion

The brief history of government performance measurement initiatives we have provided here shows a shift from almost exclusively internal, agency-directed measures of performance to a far greater emphasis on external, citizen-centered measures. While we have primarily focused on the shifts and turns in performance measurement at the federal level of government in the United States, it is certainly not a unique case. Not only, in our estimation, is this trend likely to continue but it should continue, as these kinds of measures reflect a more equal, more sovereign citizenry with greater power relative to their governments. In the next chapter, we will talk more specifically about justifications for citizen satisfaction measurement that build on many of the themes introduced in this chapter.

CHAPTER 2

The Purposes and Objectives of Citizen Satisfaction Measurement

Introduction

The last chapter closed with a discussion of the shifting focus toward external measures of government performance in an era where both consumer and citizen power has grown alongside increased access to information and knowledge of alternatives. Following a brief restatement of common (but persistent) challenges to the very foundations of citizen satisfaction measurement, this chapter provides a detailed discussion of many of the justifications, objectives, and purposes of this measurement. Here we identify numerous objectives supporting the practice of satisfaction measurement of administrative or bureaucratic institutions, along with a variety of important purposes the data can serve. Included in this list of purposes are the development of a more dynamic feedback loop connecting government and society, increased government transparency, enhanced top-down and bottom-up accountability, the rebuilding of citizen trust, effective process and service quality improvements, the facilitation of benchmarking across units of government toward identifying best practices, more efficient budgetary and resource allocation, and monitoring and motivating public employees.

Why Measure Citizen Satisfaction?

Why should governments measure the satisfaction of their citizens, clients, customers, and other stakeholders? Generally speaking, in the private sector customer satisfaction measurement is justified first and foremost on the grounds that more satisfied customers are also more loyal customers, and more loyal customers more financially profitable ones. Satisfaction measurement and management is good, in other words, for the corporate bottom line, and is thus important and intrinsically justifiable. Indeed, marketing researchers have grown increasingly focused on what they term the "marketing-finance interface," and a host of recent academic studies have confirmed the relationship between external performance metrics (such as customer satisfaction) and objective measures of corporate financial performance, such as revenue growth, profitability, stock market performance, and so on.[1]

Yet the proliferation and changing focus of performance measurement in government notwithstanding, a phenomenon we discussed near the end of the last chapter, government is decidedly dissimilar to virtually all of the companies in the private sector that measure satisfaction. As such, in most instances the objectives and purposes used to justify private sector satisfaction measurement do not apply equally well to the public sector. While companies want satisfied customers because they are more loyal customers who spend more time in their stores, spend more time browsing their websites, and/ or become more willing to buy different or more expensive products from the company, and thus ultimately spend more money on the firm's products and services, governments have no such motivation. Rarely do governments try to "up-sell" or "cross-sell" existing citizen-customers to other government services, and for many government agencies, a citizen spending a longer time on their website or a longer time at a physical location would be viewed as a sign of poor and problematic customer service, not the reverse. As such, an argument can be made that government really does not need to measure citizen satisfaction—or, even more strongly, absolutely should not waste its scarce and precious financial resources doing so.

Consider, for example, one of the most basic differences in the nature of public and private sector organizations: government does not operate in a free market, and dissatisfied citizens cannot defect to another government or a "competitive government agency" as easily as consumers in a free market can switch brands of shampoo or soda. Soda and shampoo are relatively cheap and there are many competitive alternatives, and therefore dropping one in favor of another is easy; if you don't like Coke, next time buy Pepsi, a different type of (noncola) soda altogether, or even nothing at all. Governments and government agencies, on the other hand, have a coercive monopoly over the services they provide within their own territory, and many of the "services" they offer are compulsory, not voluntary. For this reason, and adopting the language of free market economics, the "barriers to switching" are extraordinarily high when dissatisfied with a government. One way to switch—by leaving one country and seeking citizenship in another—carries heavy tangible and direct (such as the financial expense associated with taking up residence in another country) and intangible and indirect (such as the loss of an emotional attachment and a familiar language and culture) costs, and these costs typically leave citizens with little option but to remain "loyal" to their government.[2]

Given these truths about the fundamental nature of government and the alternatives (or lack thereof) most citizens have when dissatisfied, let us again ask our question: why should government measure—or even be at all concerned—about the satisfaction of its citizens? If switching costs are truly as high as suggested above, what choice do citizens have but to accept this dissatisfying experience? Indeed, if citizens could defect from governments or government agencies as easily as they switch brands of shampoo, or even simply refuse to accept the services of a government entirely, it is safe to say that the US Internal Revenue Service, and most other tax collection agencies, would have gone out of business long ago (a situation that would likely be greeted by citizens with mass celebrations, at least in the short run). But they cannot, and thus perhaps it doesn't really matter whether or not citizens are satisfied with government, or whether or not governments measure this satisfaction.

These perspectives on the questionable need for citizen satisfaction measurement with government notwithstanding, there are counterarguments suggesting that its quasi-monopoly power and high barriers to switching can actually be seen as a reason for government to engage in this activity, and that perhaps government has an even greater need to do so than the private sector. Moreover, a host of additional and useful justifications for this practice have been offered, and collectively these give us a solid idea of why this practice is not only useful, but absolutely crucial.

Developing a New Citizen-Government Feedback Loop

The preceding discussion on the different natures of the public and private sectors, and specifically the reality that citizens are less able to express dissatisfaction with government through defection, taps into a fact about government that requires a bit more elaboration. In short, this discussion provided a roundabout way of evidencing the significant limitations in a government's "exit-voice-loyalty" mechanism and, consequently, in the "feedback loops" or networks of communication connecting citizens to government.

The exit-voice-loyalty idea, first expounded in detail by economist Albert Hirschman, says that "members" of any organization have two basic options when experiencing dissatisfaction with the organization—they can "exit" (i.e., defect to an alternative supplier or organization), or they can exercise their "voice" (i.e., they can complain to the organization and hope for improvements). Because of the aforementioned barriers to exit, voice is the more relevant mechanism for citizens, the primary feedback loop connecting these two entities and allowing one to understand the nature and degree of dissatisfaction within the other. But often in citizen-government interactions voice is not exercised either, at least not in reference to the many administrative processes and services offered by the government. In many instances, citizens who are displeased with government services have been shown to neither exit nor significantly voice their dissatisfaction, but rather to withdraw and stew in their unhappiness. These citizens become passive, disconnected observers of their government who have withdrawn support without physically "exiting," rather than active supporters of the system. Consider the following evidence.

In the free market private sector, a firm or industry's complaint rate tends to be strongly related and inversely proportional to its satisfaction. That is, as consumer satisfaction with a company or industry declines, complaints tend to rise. However, this same situation does not tend to be the case for government and its administrative institutions. Indeed, given the relatively low levels of satisfaction with government, when compared to private sector industries with similarly low satisfaction,[3] one would expect far higher levels of complaints than have been observed, as figure 2.1 shows:

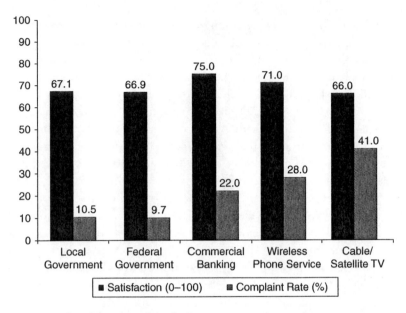

Figure 2.1 Complaint rates and satisfaction across economic sectors.
Source: American Customer Satisfaction Index, 2011.

While a low complaint rate is often thought of as a positive outcome, sometimes wrongly considered to be evidence that an organization or company is performing at a high level ("hey, no one's complaining, so we must be doing everything well!"), in reality it is not. Many corporations, for example, have gradually become aware that they are oftentimes actually better served when unhappy consumers do complain, as it allows them to identify and fix problems they might not have otherwise noticed, or not noticed until it was too late and they had lost customers. It also gives the organization an opportunity to interact with the displeased customer, and potentially repair the damaged relationship before the customer defects.[4] But even in the situation where complaints are low, hard to track, or otherwise absent, companies in competitive industries still have an advantage over government, as most of these companies can still "see" the effects of dissatisfaction as it is happening (or shortly thereafter) through customer churn and defection. Most governments and government agencies simply cannot.

In essence, government agencies are at a double disadvantage in terms of the available "feedback loops"—the two-way communication connections between citizen and government—linking them to their users, the citizens they interact with and serve. Governments are still responsible to (or in some instances, stuck with) those dissatisfied citizens who neither exercise their voice nor exit as a consequence of their dissatisfaction, but often have no idea who these folks are or why they are dissatisfied. From this perspective, private sector companies could actually be argued to have a lesser need for satisfaction measurement than the public sector, contrary to what was suggested above, as they are more likely to field complaints and can partially observe customer dissatisfaction (without actually measuring it) by virtue of their churn rate, the number of customers staying or leaving during a purchase cycle. While popular elections are a form of voice and allow citizens to express dissatisfaction with elected leaders, the administrative or bureaucratic system (our primary focus here, as we discussed in the "Introduction" and will touch on again later) is a different animal entirely, given that the individuals therein are typically appointed officials or career employees.

Therefore, satisfaction measurement—or more precisely, analyzed citizen satisfaction data—can help overcome this deficiency by providing a new network of communication connecting government and society, and a means for identifying not only the existence of, but also the sources of dissatisfaction with government experiences. For instance, governments can use satisfaction data to approximate defection levels, to determine how many citizens would, if the barriers to switching were lower, leave. They can also use this data, as we will discuss more fully over the next three chapters, to determine which processes, services, or products require improvements based on the input of the citizens themselves, much like the private sector company can improve its goods and services via the feedback given in consumer complaints. In short, citizen satisfaction data can serve as a method for both augmenting and enhancing the discourse between state and society.

Transparency and Accountability

Increasingly, democratic political systems have sought to open-up their internal processes, deliberations, and decisions to the public. This is especially true in the more advanced democracies, but this trend is apparent among many new and developing democracies as well. Over the past decade in particular, governments around the world have enacted an assortment of new "sunshine" and "right to information" laws.[5] The underlying value motivating these laws for both established and new democracies alike is, quite simply, that in a democracy everything (or very nearly everything) government does ought to be open to the inspection and scrutiny of the public. Moreover, advocates of *transparency* in government, as this principle is called, insist that for any democracy to function as it should, citizens must have access to all information relevant to their decision-making processes (for instance, prior to an election).

Accompanying this increased emphasis on transparency within democracies, and very much related to it, has been a renewed focus on *accountability*. A principle of democratic accountability demands that government and public officials must be responsible and answerable to others for their decisions, actions, and overall performance. Two basic types of democratic accountability—"top-down" and "bottom-up" accountability—are sometimes discussed in this regard. Top-down accountability refers to a situation where one unit of government (such as an administrative agency or program) is held to account and made to answer for its performance to another unit of government, such as an oversight agency or a group of elected legislators. Bottom-up accountability refers to a situation where government is made to answer to the ultimate power in a democracy, the people.

While not conceptually identical, transparency and accountability nourish one another in a democratic political system. On the one hand, access to a huge cache of publicly available information through enhanced transparency is relatively meaningless unless governments feel some obligation to answer for the decisions and actions revealed through this information. On the other hand, a government agency required and willing to answer to the people must have something to answer about, and without access to sufficient information (as gained through transparency) it is very difficult for the public to ask any (or at least the correct) questions. And to be sure, citizen satisfaction measurement and the data generated by this process can certainly help realize the goals of a more transparent and accountable government.

Satisfaction data offers a unique and meaningful piece of information for gauging how well government is performing, and for evidencing this performance to others. For instance, senior managers within government agencies can use (and have used) satisfaction data as evidence of strong performance or improvement in performance to both oversight agencies and elected legislators engaged in oversight.[6] From this perspective, the data has provided a tool for top-down accountability, to help convince both skeptical legislators and regulators that their agency is, in fact, doing a good job, or at least has identified its problems and is taking steps to correct them. Likewise from the perspective of the citizen and bottom-up accountability, satisfaction results provide an additional kind of information that gives citizens a tangible means for gauging the performance of government agencies, and perhaps demanding that these agencies answer for their performance. In the extreme, a government-wide system of satisfaction measurement—were it to be made freely available to the public—could help shape or even transform citizen perceptions of government performance as a whole, which agencies are doing a good job, are working effectively to improve their performance, and so on.

Developing Citizen Trust

The trust held collectively by a group of citizens—both in one another and in the institutions exercising power within a society—is a vital good in a democratic society. As one democratic theorist has succinctly stated, "A society that fosters robust relations of trust is probably also a society that can afford fewer regulations and greater freedoms, deal with more contingencies, tap the energy and ingenuity of its citizens, [and] limit the inefficiencies of rule-based coordination."[7] While trust cannot solve all of the ills of a democracy—and, indeed, if *perfect* trust ever existed within a society, government itself would probably be unnecessary—when citizens generally trust their government and one another, the government's job becomes considerably easier.

Yet trust (both the interpersonal and the citizens-toward-government varieties of trust) is on the decline in democracies the world over, and has been mostly heading downward for decades.[8] Citizens within many democratic systems have grown considerably less confident in the ability of their governments to perform well, to perform fairly and ethically, and to reflect the interests and needs of the citizens to whom they are ostensibly beholden.[9] This crisis of trust threatens to not only destabilize these political systems and their electoral politics, but also makes the job of government agencies increasingly difficult. Dealing with cynical citizens that come to their government experience expecting the worst is never easy.

Satisfaction measurement has something to say about the decline in trust plaguing democracies as well. For bureaucratic agencies in particular, satisfaction has been shown to be a strong determinant (or influencing factor) of citizen trust; as citizens become more satisfied with their interactions with a bureaucratic agency, they also tend to develop greater trust in both that particular agency and in the government as a whole. In later chapters, and especially chapters 4, 5, and 6, we will provide empirical evidence of this phenomenon in relation to the US federal government. But suffice it to say here, citizen satisfaction data and the examination of this data over time and across units of government can provide significant insight into the sources of trust and distrust in government—and in helping democracies go about repairing trust.

Process and Service Quality Improvements

For the most part, the first three purposes and justifications for citizen satisfaction measurement considered above—focused on creating or enhancing citizen-government communication, transparency and accountability, and citizen trust—all deal with values central to democracy, or more specifically, the relationship between a democratic government's institutions and a democratic citizenry. Starting with the role of satisfaction measurement in helping government agencies realize meaningful process or service quality improvements, the remaining objectives we consider all relate to the use of satisfaction data for decision-making processes within administrative institutions focused on improving the experiences of citizens. While the provision of better services to citizens is also vital for a democracy, to be sure, these next justifications aim more at internal initiatives relying on satisfaction data and geared toward organizational improvements and increased efficiency.

Citizen satisfaction measurement and the data gleaned from this measurement can help governments identify which agencies or programs are performing well (or poorly) from the perspective of the citizens experiencing the programs. In a sense, this is the most basic, fundamental goal of satisfaction measurement. And it is this unique informational content derived from satisfaction measurement that makes it useful for enhancing transparency and accountability, for instance. Yet when all is said and done, this information is far less meaningful if not actually learned from and acted upon. From the perspective of those working within an agency being measured, learning that the individuals you interact with are dissatisfied is important, but fixing the problems causing this dissatisfaction (with the ultimate goal of improving satisfaction) is certainly more critical. And citizen satisfaction measurement, when done correctly, can reveal not only how satisfied a group of citizens are, but also what is causing dissatisfaction and what can be done to repair it.

In the next three chapters, we will provide a variety of examples for how satisfaction data, when combined with a relatively small amount of additional survey data, can be used to identify weak spots in government services and processes, and provide direction in correcting these deficiencies. But put simply, using the data from a satisfaction survey and determining not only how satisfied citizens are, but also what factors are most (or least) important in driving or influencing that satisfaction can give public managers crucial information for determining what needs to be fixed (and conversely, those areas that if fixed would only expend resources and achieve no real increase in satisfaction). Through this kind of analysis, questions can be asked and answered that set a roadmap for reform. What is most important in driving satisfaction for a particular group of citizens? Is it interactions with frontline customer service personnel? Is it the functionality of the website? Is it the ease or accessibility of information or processes? And among this one (or these few) most important factors, which do citizens think are performing worst and thus most in need of improvements? Likewise, which improvements are most "doable" and cost effective? With answers to these and related questions, agencies are able to take the step from problem recognition to process reform, from identifying an issue (or issues) to correcting them.

Benchmarking

In the above ways, then, citizen satisfaction measurement can help public officials and government agencies better understand where their processes, services, and programs are coming up short, and where they are succeeding. Yet while this data can help institutions and actors decide where they are underperforming and where they need to do better, it can also go far beyond basic problem identification; it can help by showing agencies precisely how to get better, and does so by shedding light on the specific actions programs or agencies might take to improve in a manner that better satisfies citizens. And the most common approach for achieving this goal is to utilize citizen satisfaction data when conducting performance benchmarking.

In its current incarnation, performance benchmarking was first developed within the quality management community of the private sector.[10] The practice has become much more common in government (in conjunction with the rise in performance measurement in general discussed in the last chapter) over the past few decades. Put simply, performance benchmarking was designed, as one author has succinctly defined it, "to identify competitive targets which render the weak points of the benchmarking organization visible and to establish means of improvement."[11] Benchmarking, then, is simply a means of gaining knowledge through the art and science of comparison. And governments of all types and at all levels now undertake these kinds of comparisons toward seeking improvements. In the United States, for instance, the OMB explicitly encourages agencies to "provide the means by which their programs may be benchmarked internationally or across agencies."[12]

Performance benchmarking of citizen satisfaction results can be deemed an important activity for administrative institutions due to its usefulness in realizing two objectives. First, the ability to benchmark satisfaction data across government agencies, for instance, provides a tool for differentiating levels of performance (or incremental improvement in performance) between these agencies, and the ability to render decisions about reform priorities, or perhaps budget appropriations, on this basis. That is, the ability to benchmark and compare agencies in terms of satisfaction performance assists public officials involved in oversight functions in distinguishing the strong-performing from the poor-performing agencies, a type of benchmarking related to the principles of accountability discussed earlier.

But more importantly, at least in this context, is the ability of public managers to benchmark satisfaction data and through this to facilitate interagency learning and organizational improvement. From this perspective, the availability of satisfaction data can help agencies identify their most successful organizational counterparts (other similar agencies offering similar services, but perhaps doing a better, more satisfying job) and—through a critical comparative analysis of process or service design—adopt the "best practices" responsible for satisfaction success. That is, comparing results derived using a common metric across agencies can help agencies determine how they might improve their performance through the adoption of practices that have proven superior to their own in a similar but distinct context.

There are a large and growing number of performance benchmarks being used within many levels and types of government today. Governments now also benchmark some of their core activities and processes with private sector firms recognized as "practice leaders." Furthermore, best practices for government should increasingly be sought not only within nations, but also cross-nationally. This kind of cross-national government performance benchmarking, something we will discuss in detail in chapter 7, should serve as an imperative as the next generation of government performance measurement and benchmarking begins. As companies have come to look for best practices from global competitors, governments can certainly find much to learn from other governments as well.

Efficient Budgetary and Resource Allocation

Connected to the two objectives discussed immediately above—that government can both identify which aspects of their processes to reform toward improving satisfaction, and discover tried-and-true strategies for improving them by benchmarking with other agencies and discovering best practices—is the idea that citizen satisfaction measurement can also save money. Indeed, if you agree in principle with the importance of these two earlier objectives, it is easy to recognize how satisfaction measurement can play a significant role in limiting some (and perhaps a considerable amount) of government waste, inefficiencies borne of ill-considered reform efforts.

It seems inarguable that a significant proportion of government waste can be attributed to attempts to improve or reform government agencies, or some process or service central to those agencies, in ways that have little or no positive effect. Worse still, there are innumerable examples of government actually exacerbating problems with ill-advised, poorly conceived attempts to "make things better" (for the sake of keeping this book brief and readable, we'll eschew a detailed accounting of these instances). But thinking about the matter from the perspective of citizen satisfaction, it is easy to envision ways that even the best-intended government reformer can fail to solve (or even exacerbate) problems, if lacking certain tools and information.

Consider, for example, the case of a senior public manager that knows only that the satisfaction of the citizens interacting with her agency is low—very low, in fact—but has no additional information about why this is so. Perhaps, as is sometimes the case, this senior manager was required by regulation or legislation from higher-ups to report satisfaction to an oversight group, but for cost reasons or a general lack of interest ordered her subordinates to conduct a brief survey and measure only citizen satisfaction, and nothing else. A naïve perspective on satisfaction might advocate "fixing everything" as a solution to dissatisfaction. The logic here is simple, and even somewhat understandable—since satisfaction with the agency is very low, it makes some sense to conclude that all aspects of the agency's processes and services could use improvements, and that this slash-and-burn approach to addressing the issue is therefore warranted. Adopting this approach, resources are allocated (both money and the time and attention of employees) and aimed at addressing all potential sources of dissatisfaction, perhaps ordering website improvements, an increase in the number of customer service representatives (CSRs) and the hours they operate, a redesign of applications and forms, investing in and opening new physical locations, and so forth. Yet this approach is inefficient and wasteful, as it assumes that all of an agency's many services, processes, products, and so forth, are both equally poor and equally influential over satisfaction, assumptions that are rarely if ever correct. But if done correctly, and using some of the techniques discussed later, a citizen satisfaction survey and careful measurement can help identify the specific factor or factors that are both most influential for satisfaction and performing worse than they should. In this way, resources can be spent on only (or predominantly) the most important activities, and wasteful spending is thereby dramatically reduced.

In chapter 5, we will examine how satisfaction and related data combined with effective data modeling and tools like a "priority matrix" can help identify focal points for reform efforts and improvements. Using these relatively simple tools, government can avoid at least some wasteful resource allocation by identifying that which truly matters to citizens, that which, if improved, will effectively and efficiently increase citizen satisfaction.

Monitoring and Motivating Public Employees

Too often, the ordinary employees of a government agency—the "street-level bureaucrats," as they are sometimes called—have little notion of what the public actually thinks about them. In other cases, these street-level bureaucrats believe that the public holds an exclusively negative opinion of them, their organization, and all of the work (hard, often thankless work) that they do. The availability of citizen satisfaction data can help correct both of these informational deficiencies, and the misconceptions they spawn, as well as providing a tool for public managers to utilize in both monitoring and motivating their employees.

In the first instance, an administrative organization that has collected and analyzed satisfaction data can use this information not only to convince those involved in oversight that the agency is doing a good job, as we discussed earlier, but also to show its employees that they are doing a good job, that their work is appreciated, and that their efforts are bearing fruit. In many cases, this data can radically alter perceptions among employees about how they are viewed; in fact, satisfaction data often paints a picture considerably different—and far more positive—than what these employees anticipate. Because satisfaction data is often collected specifically from those citizens that have actually experienced an agency, its personnel, and/or its processes and services, a point we will elaborate on in the next chapter, these "actual consumers" tend to have far more positive perceptions of an agency than the general public, who may know little more about an agency than what they hear in the news (which most often involves a scandal, misspent funds, budget deficits, and so on). Furthermore, many street-level bureaucrats only have the opportunity to interact with citizens when something has gone wrong (such as a CSR fielding complaints or offering assistance to a disgruntled citizen, an official managing tax or other regulatory audits, a CSR working with citizens who have been denied government benefits or loans, etc.), and thus mistakenly believe that all of their customers share the negative opinions of this select few.

From another angle, by providing public managers with data rating particular aspects of agency performance, such as the satisfaction of citizens that have contacted a call center, filed an application, or requested information, these managers can use this data to monitor and track how frontline employees are succeeding or coming up short. If succeeding, this information can be used to motivate and congratulate these employees. If doing worse than expected, this data can allow managers to recognize this substandard performance early along, perhaps retrain or reassign employees, establish new training protocols, and/or establish new standards and performance goals that can motivate employees to boost their performance in the future (see table 2.1).

Table 2.1 A summary of objectives/purposes of citizen satisfaction measurement

Satisfaction Measurement Objective	Summary
Citizen-Government Feedback Loop	Provide a feedback loop helpful in identifying the existence and the sources of dissatisfaction with government
Transparency and Accountability	Make performance information more available to citizens, and government more answerable to citizens and other public officials
Citizen Trust	Improve citizen trust in the performance of government
Quality Improvements	Help government identify and improve those aspects of services most important to citizens
Benchmarking	Help government identify benchmarking partners and best practices useful in achieving improvements
Budgetary Allocations	Help government invest resources in the areas most in need of improvement
Motivate Public Employees	Monitor the performance of public employees; motivate and manage employees with insight into successes and information about shortcomings

Conclusion

In sum, and as we have suggested throughout this chapter, there are many purposes, objectives, and justifications available that support public organizations' decision to perform satisfaction measurement. While these objectives differ from those of private sector companies to some extent, they are just as vital nonetheless. Whether it is to develop new government-citizen feedback loops and networks of communication connecting these two groups, increase transparency, accountability and/or citizen trust, improve process and service quality, or for any of the other purposes discussed above, citizen satisfaction measurement can and should play a prominent role in government performance measurement. The next chapter begins the process of illuminating how citizen satisfaction measurement can be undertaken.

CHAPTER 3

The Practice of Citizen Satisfaction Measurement: Unit of Analysis Selection, Questionnaire Design, and Data Collection

Introduction

In the last chapter we examined the "why" question, outlining a series of purposes and objectives underpinning the practice of citizen satisfaction measurement. In this chapter and the next, we turn to the "how" question (or more accurately, questions) and examine some techniques and methods utilized in citizen satisfaction measurement, ultimately providing a step-by-step review of the most basic issues that should be addressed when beginning (or updating, transforming, or refashioning) a satisfaction measurement program. Predominantly nontechnical in nature, at least where possible, and thus hopefully accessible to both experienced practitioners and those new to the field, this discussion offers a look at the major phases of the satisfaction measurement process, including selection of the level or institution of government to measure, identification of the population or segment to measure, the identification and selection of key factors that influence citizen satisfaction (drivers) and factors that are influenced by satisfaction (outcomes), operationalization of the citizen satisfaction concept, development of a survey questionnaire, and data collection. In the next chapter, we continue this discussion by examining and comparing some analytical and statistical modeling techniques. Finally, in chapter 5 we show how this data, once collected and analyzed, can be interpreted in an action-oriented way toward identifying foci for improvements aimed at stronger citizen satisfaction performance.

Measuring Citizen Satisfaction

In the sections that follow, and truly, in the two chapters that follow this one, we are primarily interested in gaining a better understanding of how governments and government agencies, and more specifically the research practitioners employed therein—in addition to a range of other potentially interested parties, such as watchdog groups, academics, or independent researchers—can go about accurately and reliably measuring the satisfaction of citizens, and optimally using the data produced through this process. By necessity, we will need to skip some of the detail involved in this measurement, such as some of the steps involved in questionnaire design, some of the considerations required for data collection, or the full range of statistical procedures utilized. The inclusion of this material would result in a much longer, much different, and much less accessible book. In a sense, what follows is more a "primer" on citizen satisfaction measurement than a fully detailed "how-to manual." Nevertheless, this discussion should provide the inexperienced practitioner (and refresh the experienced one) with the major issues and questions that should be addressed when implementing a satisfaction measurement system.

Choosing the Level and Institution of Government to Measure

Throughout the preceding material, and likewise in most of the material that follows, we have focused first and foremost on citizen satisfaction measurement of administrative or bureaucratic institutions. For reasons mentioned in both the "Introduction" and in chapter 1, this approach is justified; no set of institutions has a greater need for satisfaction measurement than government bureaucracy, precisely because these institutions lack the mechanisms that allow citizens to voice their displeasure through elections. Yet this should not end all discussion on the matter, as there are certainly reasons for measuring satisfaction with a range of distinct levels and types of governmental institutions—those comprised of elected, appointed, and career political actors alike. Thus, before proceeding, let us consider some of the other institutions where satisfaction measurement could be conducted, before coming full circle and reiterating the importance of focusing this type of measurement on bureaucratic institutions.

In a political system such as the United States, and likewise in most contemporary democracies around the world today, governments are highly complex, multilayered entities. These systems typically contain multiple distinct spheres of power, each with some degree of autonomous authority. Because of this, the issue of "what" to measure citizen satisfaction with is decidedly more complex in these constitutional democracies. That is, while it would certainly make satisfaction measurement considerably easier, the days of the all-powerful dictator, who aggressively hordes all power and authority and confers it upon himself, are mostly a thing of the past. (All other things being equal, satisfaction measurement of an absolute dictator would be relatively easy—at least from the perspective of which "institution" to measure—as only one actor holds any real authority in such a system. The dictator's willingness to allow such measurement is another matter entirely, and I, personally, would not want to be the statistician tasked with telling said dictator that his satisfaction rating had dropped.) Most democracies, on the other hand, rest on constitutional systems that outline distinct levels of government (local, state/provincial, and central/national) founded in the principles of federalism and divided power. Moreover, each of these levels of government is typically comprised of functionally separate institutions, such as executive, legislative, judicial, and administrative branches, complicating the matter further.

Without exception, there are reasons to advocate satisfaction measurement of any and all of the levels and institutions of government existing within most modern democracies. Citizen satisfaction measurement has, for instance, been done at the federal, state, and local levels of government in the United States, yet has focused almost exclusively (as we are here) on the administrative apparatuses within each of these different levels. There has been a wealth of satisfaction research related to local government services over the past four-plus decades, focused on things such as fire protection, waste disposal, and police services.[1] State government-related research has measured satisfaction with some of the most prominent citizen-facing bureaucracies and services at that level, such as tax collection agencies, highways, and departments of motor vehicles.[2] And as we will see in the chapters that follow, US federal departments, agencies, and programs of all shapes and sizes have been the subject of satisfaction measurement as well.[3]

But beyond these most common measures of citizen satisfaction with administrative or bureaucratic agencies across levels of government, there exist good reasons for measuring satisfaction with a range of additional types of governmental and political institutions—both formal and informal—regardless of the level of government in which we are primarily interested. Starting with the informal, satisfaction measurement of political parties or large, organized interest groups (such as the National Rifle Association or Planned Parenthood) could give these organizations clearer insight into their success or failure in attracting new or maintaining old members. As these organizations operate more like private sector entities and attempt to both win new and maintain old "loyal customers," this kind of measurement could prove highly useful. Indeed, collecting and modeling satisfaction data with political parties and interest groups could more closely approximate how this work is done vis-à-vis private sector firms, in terms of the content and objectives of the research, and the recent adoption by many political parties of the marketing techniques of private sector entities (such as targeting, advertising, customer relationship management, and direct mailing) would seem to lend support to this suggestion.[4]

Likewise, satisfaction research focused on the performance of an elected legislative body or individual elected legislators (such as the US Congress and its members), or the institutions surrounding an elected executive (such as state governors or the office of the president of the United States), could also yield very useful insights. The US Congress is consistently considered one of the least popular institutions in the country, and presidents and other executives often struggle to maintain popularity or identify the causes of flagging popularity, and satisfaction measurement aimed at discovering and addressing the sources of satisfaction and/or dissatisfaction with these institutions could prove valuable as well.

Yet satisfaction measurement is less needed for both these informal and elected formal institutions, and for several reasons. First, formal elective institutions are already subjected to a huge quantity of public opinion polling, making the addition of new measures (no matter how much more rigorous) less necessary. There is no shortage of studies revealing public discontent with Congress, which has (at the time we are writing) been at or near its historically lowest levels, and daily tracking studies of approval for the US president are conducted by innumerable research groups and media outlets.[5] Second, and as we discussed in the last chapter, these formal institutions are comprised of elected officials (or mostly elected officials), and elections serve as a form of "consumer voice" that makes satisfaction measurement less urgent, while organizations like parties and interest groups are able to gauge their consumer satisfaction through objective indicators like their fluctuating membership numbers, donations received, and electoral success for the issues they care about. In these cases, the feedback loops connecting citizen and government are already well established through the democratic process, while virtually no such mechanisms exist for administrative institutions, a fact that (in part) had led many to claim that the modern bureaucracy is excessively insulated, detached from the societies they provide services to, and suffering from a "democratic deficit"[6] and/or a "crisis of legitimacy."[7] Many government agencies also offer goods and services at least somewhat more similar to those offered by the private sector than elective institutions tasked with setting policy, further validating satisfaction measurement and modeling techniques like those used in the private sector.

Therefore, while throughout the remainder of the text we will focus predominantly on satisfaction measurement of administrative institutions, this is not to say that these and only these institutions are legitimate foci for this kind of measurement. Citizen satisfaction measurement has potentially useful applications across the full range of institutions comprising most modern political systems.

Choosing the Agency, Population, or Segment of Citizens for Measurement

Reaffirming the importance of measuring satisfaction with administrative or bureaucratic institutions simplifies the next issue that needs to be addressed, at least to some extent: choosing the *population* of citizens with which to measure satisfaction. Obviously, if we are particularly focused on citizen satisfaction with administrative institutions, we will interview and measure the satisfaction of a *sample* of those citizens (or customers, clients, or stakeholders) that relate in some way to these institutions.[8] Yet this does not entirely answer the question either. Virtually every government in existence today has a sizeable number of administrative departments, each responsible for administering some particular category of laws or enforcing some set of executive or legislative mandates. Each of these departments typically has authority over several distinct agencies, and these agencies usually administer several programs each. An individual program will often provide different services (or benefits, or regulatory processes) to several discrete groups of citizens, each of which could be considered a unique population for satisfaction measurement. In short, depending on which department, agency, program, and service we are interested in focusing our research on, different populations of citizens might be targeted for satisfaction measurement.

To be sure, then, narrowing the object of citizen satisfaction measurement to the extremely broad category that is "administrative institutions" clarifies the population to be chosen for measurement and interviewed only slightly. Among all these departments, agencies, programs, and offices, which citizen-users should be interviewed and measured in a satisfaction study? If, to give just one example, we happened to be tasked with measuring citizen satisfaction with the US Department of Justice and are given no further guidance, we would have to decide which of its four leadership offices, eight divisions, six agencies, twenty-nine offices, two commissions, one bureau, one center, and one task force to focus on. Should we interview citizens who have experienced any one of these units? What about citizens who have experienced or interacted with several of them? Are some of these units more relevant for measuring citizen satisfaction with than others? A few further examples might help clarify the difficulties involved in the population-of-measurement determination process.

Let's start with a simple case, and then proceed to a tougher one. Let us assume we have been tasked with measuring satisfaction with a particular service offered by one program within one administrative agency. The potential group of citizens we could interview and measure satisfaction with—the population—will be relatively well-defined in this instance. Indeed, it may be possible to proceed by just collecting a representative random sample (a concept we mention in the footnote above and will investigate more when discussing data collection) of that entire population of citizens without distinction; anyone who has come into contact with that service offered by that agency is a potential respondent to our survey. That is, if the program is largely undifferentiated (it offers just that one basic service to each and every citizen it interacts with) and has only one significant contact point (for instance, its call center), then we may only need to measure the satisfaction of citizens that have experienced the program's services through its call center. In this instance, our population is determinate, concrete, and finite—anyone that has experienced the agency's services and used its call center (perhaps over some predetermined time period) is a potentially valid respondent—and we are left only with devising a means for collecting a random sample from among this population and interviewing these individuals about their perceptions using our survey instrument.

In a vast majority of cases, however, the matter is not nearly so simple. For virtually every administrative department, most agencies, and many programs, different citizens can experience very different processes or services and come into contact with these services in innumerable ways. In this more complex "real world" of survey research, one approach might be to attempt to measure all of the citizen-customers of the agency or program as discrete subgroups each requiring separate analysis, perhaps divided by their specific type of contact with the program. For instance, one subsample might contain respondents who have used the website, another those that have spoken with a CSR in the contact center, a third those that visited a physical location, a fourth those that have used all of these contact points, and so on. Or, we might divide the population by the differential nature of the delivered service or process, and treat those that have filed Application A, those that have filed Application B, and those that that filed both A and B (but not C or D) as separate subgroups. However, each of these approaches is certain to be more costly—in terms of both data collection costs and the labor involved in analysis—and if taken to an extreme, probably prohibitively so. In short, both the burdens of analysis and the costs of data collection make the "measure it all, let the statistician sort it out" approach to satisfaction measurement less attractive.

While the question of which group of citizen-users within a program, agency, or department to target for measurement—or conversely, which particular program, agency, or department to measure satisfaction with—will often be a tricky one, as the above examples show, and while no universally correct guidance can be given to entirely eliminate these complexities, a few important guidelines are available for the manager or research practitioner when addressing this issue.

First, measure satisfaction with an agency or program that is *citizen-facing*, that has substantial and regular interaction with a significant number of citizen-users. While this may seem like a trivial or intuitive consideration, it is often overlooked during the planning phase of a citizen satisfaction measurement project. Indeed, although it can tempting to measure the perceptions of every possible citizen vis-à-vis every imaginable government program, many have very little actual contact with the citizen population at large, and thus the results of any survey measuring perceptions with such an agency will reflect only (at best) partially informed opinion that can offer little in the way of useful information for process or service improvements.

By way of example, the Internal Revenue Service (IRS) and the Transportation Security Administration (TSA) are two instances of citizen-facing agencies that many (or even most) Americans have had some actual experience and contact with, through the tax-filing process and the airport security screening process, respectively. Through these services, a large number of citizens can (or are required) to visit actual websites to experience services firsthand, call-into contact centers, interact with street-level bureaucrats face-to-face, fill out applications and other paperwork, and so forth, making these agencies "citizen-facing." On the other hand, the Department of Defense's Missile Defense Agency is a poor example of a citizen-facing agency, as it is an organization that very, very few Americans have had any direct experience with, although many may have opinions about the objective of its mission and work. But as we have emphasized throughout the book to this point, one central goal of citizen satisfaction measurement is to use these results to identify reform priorities and positively affect internal process or service improvements toward increasing satisfaction, and citizens who only have opinions of a program without actual experience can offer little real insight to this end. In short, there is a difference between *policy* (which citizens may have opinions on, but which is constitutionally defined as something to be made by elected representatives) and the processes and services citizens directly experience, and measuring satisfaction with the latter is typically vastly more useful.

Secondly, once the citizen-facing agency or agencies have been chosen for satisfaction measurement, it is best to sample and interview only citizens that have had some *actual experience and direct contact* with the agency or program under investigation, at least if one of the goals of the measurement project is to provide guidance on how these institutions might improve their processes and services (and satisfaction). That is, in order to use satisfaction data to identify poor-performing areas that might lead to improved satisfaction if reformed, the researcher is best served by interviewing citizens who have actually experienced those processes or services, and we thus need to first identify and select for interviewing only those citizens who have had actual (as well as, typically, somewhat recent) experience with the agency.[9] Nevertheless, there is a not-totally-unreasonable position that says that all citizens should be measured about every government program or agency—even those they have had absolutely no contact or direct experience with—in a democratic system, as most programs are funded from the general pool of tax dollars, and thereby "impact" all citizens, even if only indirectly. This idea notwithstanding, for a large majority of satisfaction studies, choosing actual citizen-users for interviewing is preferable, precisely because the data collected and the information gleaned from it will be far more useful for devising reform strategies.

Third, choose for measurement a group of citizens, or a process or service used by a group of citizens, that you *suspect may be dissatisfied/dissatisfying*, as improvements in satisfaction for this group may be more impactful and useful. Senior managers and others within agencies often have a sense regarding some group's dissatisfaction, perhaps due to a higher volume of complaints or a lower success rate in getting the group to comply with agency rules and regulations.

Similarly, a larger regulatory burden, a more involved paperwork completion process, or a longer time taken by the agency in processing the applications/forms completed by this group may lead the manager or researcher to suspect lower levels of satisfaction among these users. Yet regardless of the way this knowledge is arrived at, many public managers have a general sense for which group of citizens may be the least satisfied, and this qualitative, experienced-based knowledge can (and often does) drive the decision-making process regarding which citizens to include for measurement. And because a group of dissatisfied citizens may be responsible for "dragging-down" the average satisfaction of an entire population of citizens, targeting this group for measurement at least initially, and for subsequent efforts aimed at improvement, is often a sound and resource-efficient strategy.

Fourth, choose an *important subsegment of citizen-users* of the program's processes or services for satisfaction measurement. The word "important" is, of course, a loaded term in this context, as one of the basic precepts of the delivery of fair and impartial administrative services in a democratic society is that all citizens are "equally important" (or at least equal) in the eyes of the bureaucracy. But certainly, at least as far as the provision of administrative services and the quality and satisfaction delivered by those services is concerned, some citizens *are* more important than others. Not only, as mentioned above, are some groups of citizens less satisfied than others due to the nature of their interactions with an agency (and thus a more important focus in terms of satisfaction improvement efforts), but some subgroups of citizens experiencing a program require a greater portion of that program's budget, are numerically larger relative to the total group of citizens interacting with an agency, have more frequent or more involved interactions with the agency, and so forth. In these ways, making distinctions between different categories of citizens is warranted, as is determining which group of citizens to measure based on these kinds of distinctions.

Yet all of these recommendations notwithstanding, probably the most important guidance that can be given here is that it is vital to choose what (or whom) to measure carefully and to avoid "paralysis by analysis," where too much or poorly defined data prevents careful, effective, and action-oriented analysis of results. Perhaps the only sin greater than not measuring and working to improve the satisfaction of your citizen-user population at all is measuring it and doing nothing with the knowledge acquired, and well-planned satisfaction measurement can help avoid this transgression.

Identifying Key Drivers and Outcomes of Citizen Satisfaction

Once we have decided on a citizen-facing administrative department (or agency, program, service, etc.)—and a directly experienced and "important" group of citizens that interact with this organization—to measure satisfaction with, we must next decide how best to measure the perceptions of these citizens. More specifically, at this stage we must decide which aspects of the agency's processes or services are most relevant for measurement alongside satisfaction, in terms of those elements of the experience that are most likely to *significantly drive or influence citizen satisfaction* (i.e., cause satisfaction to increase or decline) and serve as *relevant and important outcomes of satisfaction*. While this process is related to both questionnaire/survey design (discussed below) and the statistical analysis of data (discussed in the next chapter), it is both a logically and practically distinct issue that should be considered first.

As mentioned on several occasions thus far, and especially in chapter 2, citizen satisfaction data can be important and useful in and of itself, absent any additional supporting data. That is, knowing how satisfied a group of citizens are with their experiences with an administrative agency can help legislators or others judge and compare bureaucratic performance, while also helping citizens hold all of these actors accountable for their performance. But another objective of this kind of measurement is to help agencies make internal decisions that lead to improved services that in turn provide stronger user satisfaction, while also offering a clearer picture of the tangible consequences (or benefits) of increasing or declining satisfaction. And without knowing why satisfaction is, for instance, lower than expected or declining over time, these tasks are difficult, if not impossible. For these reasons, when designing a questionnaire aimed at measuring citizen satisfaction it is essential to first identify and then include items in a questionnaire asking the respondent to rate activities that influence satisfaction (these perceptions and questionnaire items we will sometimes call "drivers" of satisfaction below) along with items that are driven or influenced by satisfaction (sometimes also called "outcomes").[10] Let's begin by examining drivers of satisfaction, aspects of an agency experience likely to influence satisfaction.

Identifying relevant drivers and outcomes of citizen satisfaction is a qualitative process, one that requires the participation of individuals with intimate knowledge of the internal workings of the agency and its processes and services, and sometimes also the participation of consumers in open-ended interviews or qualitative interviews, focus groups, and so forth. It also varies somewhat widely across organizations. While driver identification would be decidedly easier if all agencies worked in roughly the same way, this is simply not the case. Agencies interface with their customers in a variety of different ways regarding an equally wide variety of processes and services. Given these realities, the factors that drive or influence satisfaction tend to differ across agencies and programs, and between some agencies these differences are stark.

The one factor that can help group agencies together is a common or similar core mission. For example, two agencies tasked with providing benefits that interface with their customers mostly through a benefits application and a benefits qualification decision-making process, or through the actual delivery of these benefits (via regular checks sent through the mail or electronic funds transfers, for instance), may both deem similar (or even identical) drivers of satisfaction to be appropriate in their measurement system. Likewise, two service-providing agencies, both primarily tasked with offering free information to the public through websites, the mail, brochures, and related means, might settle on very similar drivers of satisfaction. Yet even when dealing with agencies delivering very similar services or administering similar processes, slight idiosyncratic differences between these agencies may lead to the conclusion that satisfaction is driven by different means, and thus requires the measurement of different drivers.

These aforementioned considerations notwithstanding, and using experience and prior research as our guide, a few drivers that have often been identified by researchers as important factors influencing citizen satisfaction with a large cross-section of agencies are listed below. These include:

1. *Information Delivery*: Many government agencies are primarily responsible for delivering some type of information to the public. Other agencies are tasked with a very different core mission (such as the enforcement of regulations), yet still must deliver information as a central part of these tasks. Given this, asking citizens to rate some number of questions measuring the *completeness, quality, timeliness, clarity*, or *accessibility of the agency's information* can often serve as drivers of satisfaction that work well in predicting satisfaction for many government agencies.

2. *Process:* Often both regulatory and benefits-delivering agencies, as well as a handful of service-delivering agencies, require citizens they come into contact with to complete some standard process, such as completing paperwork evidencing compliance with regulatory standards or applying for benefits. For these agencies, measuring the *ease, clarity, and accessibility of forms*, and/or the *efficiency* or *timeliness of completing a process* are often relevant drivers of satisfaction.

3. *Website:* Given the explosive growth of e-government over the past decade (a phenomenon we discuss more fully in chapter 6), virtually every government agency now relies on its website as a vital part of its interface with citizens. For many and even most agencies, therefore, the *ease of navigation, clarity of information, usefulness of information*, and/or *the speed and usefulness of search results* delivered by a website can provide important drivers of satisfaction.

4. *Customer Service:* While websites have allowed many agencies to downsize the number of call centers and CSRs working within their agencies, the customer service provided through these centers is still a central part of many citizens' experiences with government agencies. Thus, the *professionalism, courtesy, efficiency,* or *knowledge of call center CSRs* remain important features driving satisfaction for many agencies and programs.

Turning now to outcomes of satisfaction, and just as all agencies are unlikely to deem an identical set of drivers of satisfaction to be relevant to their interactions with citizens, agencies are also likely to determine that different outcomes of satisfaction are most relevant, and have an interest in knowing how diverse future perceptions or behaviors are influenced by increasing (or declining) satisfaction. For instance, we mentioned in chapter 2 the value of satisfaction as a driver of trust in the government as a whole. While some agencies may be interested in their organization's role in driving trust in government writ large, others may have a lesser interest in this kind of trust (which is a relatively abstract concept) than in a more concrete, tangible outcome. Some agencies, such as regulatory agencies, may be most interested in the relationship between citizen satisfaction with a process or service they provide and compliance with the regulations their agency is attempting to enforce. A variety of agencies may be interested in the relationship between satisfaction and positive word-of-mouth, especially for a newer service (such as e-government or the electronic delivery of benefits) that the agency is attempting to prod citizens toward. With this in mind, a few of the outcomes of citizen satisfaction that may work well for agencies are listed below.

1. *Trust or Confidence*: The importance of citizen trust to the functioning of a democratic government was discussed in the last chapter, and is something we will cover in greater detail later. But for many agencies, and especially those agencies that come into contact with a large cross-section of a national or local population, the impact of satisfaction on citizen trust—which can be measured as the *general degree of trust in the political system as a whole* and/or the *trust (or confidence) in the particular agency experienced*—can prove a vital outcome measure.

2. *Loyalty*: While governments often have a monopoly on the goods and services they offer, in some instances, like the case of local government we mentioned earlier, this is not so. Sometimes agencies also offer multiple methods for experiencing a service (e.g., a website versus paper forms or call centers) that "compete" internally for the business of citizens. And where competition does exist for an agency or government (from either the private sector or another government or government agency), measuring the loyalty of existing citizen-customers—through

such items as *repurchase intention* or *intention to reuse*—may be useful.

3. *Compliance*: Many regulatory agencies are focused primarily on convincing (or coercing) citizens to comply with the regulations the agency is tasked with enforcing. For these agencies, measuring the relationship between satisfaction and compliance— such as the respondent's *intention of following rules* or *accurately and truthfully completing required documentation*—can serve as useful outcome measures.

4. *Recommendation or Word-of-Mouth*: Just like private sector companies, government agencies often attempt to transition citizen-users from receiving goods and services using one means to another—such as shifting those citizens accustomed to contacting a call center to a website—as a cost-savings measure. In these instances, measuring the respondent's *likelihood to say positive things about an experience* or their *likelihood of recommending the service to others* can provide insight into how successful (or fast) these efforts will prove.

5. *Complaints*: While citizens often complain to government at far lower rates than do customers of private sector companies, measuring complaint rates, or whether the user *has complained recently about their experience with the agency*, and if so, *how well that complaint was handled*, can nevertheless provide useful information. In particular, this outcome measure can clarify how improving satisfaction is likely to lead to fewer complaints, and in turn lower the cost of complaint handling and recovery.

While obviously these lists of both drivers and outcomes of citizen satisfaction are partial, and while unique agencies or programs might require drivers or outcomes different than anything we have highlighted here, these examples provide a solid foundation for deciding what to measure along with citizen satisfaction in a questionnaire. Regardless, to maximize the usefulness of the information gleaned through a satisfaction measurement system, the practitioner involved in designing their agency's system must pay considerable attention to selecting these drivers and outcomes. Below we will outline some additional considerations entailed in questionnaire construction, and in chapter 4, we discuss in greater detail how drivers of satisfaction, satisfaction, and outcomes of satisfaction can be statistically modeled and linked together in a manner useful for making critical operational decisions aimed at improving satisfaction in as efficient a manner as possible.

Operationalizing Citizen Satisfaction

Having now considered the importance of identifying drivers and outcomes of satisfaction that the researcher can and should include in his or her questionnaire alongside satisfaction, we turn to some challenges and issues involved in measuring the satisfaction concept, before proceeding to discuss questionnaire development. Not surprisingly, given the long history of research on this topic across several academic disciplines, there are multiple and sometimes competing views on how researchers ought to *operationalize* (i.e., create an effective survey question for measuring) satisfaction. Thus, and as we have been forced to do with a few other topics to this point, we will provide an only-partial exposition of these diverse approaches to creating a satisfaction survey question.[11] More specifically, we will primarily deal here with three core, perennial issues involved when creating a satisfaction survey question, before offering some recommendations regarding the matter: how to craft and word a survey item that most accurately captures the respondent's "true" level of satisfaction (with as little error as possible); whether satisfaction should be treated as a cumulative or a transactional phenomenon; and, regardless of the answer to these first two questions, whether satisfaction should be asked as a binary, a categorical, or a continuous variable.

There are many, many ways that researchers—academics and practitioners alike—have operationalized and measured satisfaction in research studies over the past 50+ years. Indeed, in some early studies attempts were made to gauge satisfaction indirectly through distinct but ostensibly related observable phenomena,[12] like customer defections (churn rate) or complaint behavior. That is, if customers aren't complaining or leaving the organization for a competitor, on this logic, then they must be satisfied, and all we need to do to gauge satisfaction is measure these related, but more easily observed phenomena. But as we have already illustrated in chapter 2, this logic works quite poorly in relation to government services, as even highly dissatisfied citizens tend to complain at low levels to the government (a phenomenon we elaborate on in chapter 6), and because defection to a competitor is virtually impossible in most instances in this context.

These early efforts notwithstanding, more recent satisfaction researchers have attempted to capture the survey respondent's satisfaction in one of just a few ways, based on their position on one or a few theories of satisfaction: to ask the respondent directly the level of his or her satisfaction with a consumption experience ("how satisfied are you?"); to infer satisfaction based on how well the experience met (or exceeded, or fell short of) expectations ("did the experience fall short of, meet, or exceed your expectations?"); or to measure a concept thought definitive of satisfaction, but one that does not directly ask the respondent to indicate their satisfaction per se (such as asking about the respondent's "pleasure," "happiness," or "delight" with an experience). Examples of some of these types of question are provided in the next section, and our perspective on the matter is offered at the end of this section.

In addition to the issue of how precisely to word a question asking consumers about their satisfaction, additional debate revolves around whether it is best to ask the respondent about overall satisfaction across a set of experiences occurring on a longer timeline and over multiple occasions (cumulative satisfaction), or to ask about satisfaction with just one particular encounter with a good or service (transactional satisfaction). While transaction-specific measures of satisfaction, which usually ask the consumer to rate only their "most recent experience" with a good or service, have some validity and usefulness—especially if an organization is interested in receiving consumer feedback about a very particular process or service at a specific moment in time and comparing it with earlier or later perceptions (for instance, is contacting the IRS on tax day more or less satisfying than contacting it three months earlier or later?), most researchers tend to favor cumulative measures of satisfaction. While several reasons for defending this position exist—including the basic argument that, for the most part, researchers find greater operational value in knowing about a broad array of experiences over a longer timeline than a single, perhaps idiosyncratic experience—research has shown that cumulative measures of satisfaction, precisely because they do capture a broader range of consumer experiences and attitudes, more successfully relate to and predict outcome measures like customer loyalty, future consumption behavior, trust, and so forth.[13]

Finally, while to some extent a settled debate, at least in the academic literature, some disagreement still remains about whether satisfaction should be asked as a binary, "yes-no" question—wherein the respondent can select only one or the other option, implying either nonexistent or perfect satisfaction and nothing in between—or rather as a categorical or semi-continuous variable, where a range of options are available along a numerical scale (possibly with verbal cues) that the respondent can select. Examples of the former approach can be seen in virtually every television commercial boasting of a company's strong customer relationships. But adorable lizards notwithstanding, most satisfaction researchers would put little stock in an insurance company's claim of "97% satisfaction," and the major flaw in this approach is that it treats satisfaction too rigidly and simplistically, rather than as an individual cognitive-psychological phenomenon that exists on a broader continuum from low to high.[14] Thus, virtually every research study in this area rejects treating satisfaction as a dichotomous variable and chooses instead to measure it either on a Likert scale—where, on a 5-point scale, for example, options like "very dissatisfied," "somewhat dissatisfied," "neutral," "somewhat satisfied," and "very satisfied" will be available to the respondent—or as a quasi-continuous variable, where, using a 1–10 scale as an example, the respondent can select one of the extremes (1="very dissatisfied" and 10="very satisfied"), or any numeric option in between.

In sum, and based on a thorough review of the literature and substantial experience conducting research on the topic, satisfaction is, in our estimation, best treated as a cumulative phenomenon (i.e., measured as satisfaction with the sum total of experiences with the program or agency, rather than just the most recent experience), and with the question (or questions) in the survey asked on a quasi-continuous (such as a 1–10) or a categorical Likert-type scale, rather than as a yes-or-no binary variable. Furthermore, and as we will illustrate in the next chapter, rather than selecting a single survey question and relying on it alone to reflect the "true" level of the respondents' (in the aggregate) satisfaction, a method that implies that satisfaction itself is unidimensional and can be measured by a single variable without error (a dubious suggestion), many researchers opt instead to measure the concept as a *multivariate latent variable*. On this approach, the researcher collects data on several interrelated survey questions tapping-into the respodent's satisfaction (perhaps including all of the alternative types of satisfaction questions mentioned earlier) and models these together during statistical analysis, an analytical method that often provides data that more precisely predicts outcomes and minimizes random error variance (noise) in the data. We provide examples of the questions that might be included in this kind of latent satisfaction variable below, and in the next chapter we provide more detail on how (statistically) one can model these questions together as a latent variable.

Constructing a Citizen Satisfaction Questionnaire

Entire books can and have been written on the subject of the design of questionnaires used in survey research. The wording used in questions, the ratings scales used to measure the opinions or perceptions elicited through the questions, the cues or anchors used to guide respondents when answering, the treatment of nonresponses and refusals, the ideal length of an interview, and literally dozens of other difficult issues arise when designing such a questionnaire. It would be far outside the scope and central subject of this book to address all of these issues here, and many very useful works on the topic already exist.[15] Regardless, a few key issues relating to survey design are worth mentioning at this point.

First, it is almost always the case that shorter is better when it comes to designing a survey, in terms of the total number of questions and the total time needed for the average respondent to complete the interview. Yet sometimes researchers—and more often the managers overseeing a research project—become fixated on adding an ever-growing number of questions to a survey, viewing it as an opportunity to answer any and all lingering questions about their department or agency, regardless of the direct relevance of these matters to citizen satisfaction. But whether collected over the telephone, the Internet, face-to-face, or via the mail, the completion rate for a questionnaire (the percentage of potential respondents that actually complete the survey), and ultimately the quality of the data collected through it, is almost always inversely proportional to the amount of time it takes the respondent to complete the questionnaire.[16] Because getting each respondent to fully complete a questionnaire once they begin yields more usable and more reliable data, resisting attempts to create a questionnaire that "asks everything" is vital.

Second, short, clear, concise, and carefully crafted questions that tap specifically into the phenomenon or activity of interest tend to be more successful than longer and more complex questions. A few examples of this type of concise and focused question are provided below (see table 3.1), examples taken from a survey measuring satisfaction with the US federal government. While it is often tempting to "cram" each question with as much information as possible, just like it is tempting to add as many questions to the survey as possible, longer and more complex questions often result in two related difficulties. First, longer questions that contain multiple features or concepts (for instance, asking a respondent to rate "the ease of use, clarity of information, completeness of information, and quality of search results of website X" in a single question) are more difficult for the respondent to answer, as they are forced to somehow rate all of these diverse elements of the website at once. And since a website could conceivably provide excellent search results and be very easy to use, while at the same time containing unclear and incomplete information, the respondent may be at a loss for how to respond accurately. Moreover, even if the respondent does somehow answer a question like that posed above, how is the researcher to interpret this information? If the resulting score is low, does that mean that the respondent is unhappy with all or just some of those aspects of the website? And if only unhappy with some, how does the researcher determine which ones? In short, very little actionable information aimed at improvement can be gleaned from complex, imprecise, convoluted questions. For these reasons, short and concise questions focusing on a single idea (or, at most, perhaps two closely interrelated concepts) are to be preferred, as these are less burdensome for the respondent and produce more easily interpretable data for the researcher.

Third, while this relates in part to a particular type of statistical modeling often done on citizen satisfaction data (an approach mentioned above that we outline in the next chapter), it is normally the case that "multiple-item measures" are to be preferred over single-item measures. We hinted at the nature of these types of measures when examining drivers and outcomes of satisfaction, as well

Table 3.1 Sample questions for a citizen satisfaction questionnaire

Sample Question	Question Wording
Courtesy	How courteous were the the Agency's personnel (CSRs)? Using a 10 point scale on which "1" means "not at all courteous" and "10" means "very courteous," how courteous were the Agency's personnel?
Timeliness	How timely and efficient was the Agency in administering the process you experienced? Using a 10 point scale on which "1" means "not timely and efficient" and "10" means "very timely and efficient," how timely and efficient was the Agency in administering the process you experienced?
Website Usability	How logically organized and easy to navigate is the Agency's website? Using a 10 point scale on which "1" means "not logically organized and difficult to navigate" and "10" means "very well organized and easy to navigate," how logically organized and easy to navigate is the Agency's website?
Overall Satisfaction	First, please consider all your experiences to date with the Agency's services. Using a 10 point scale on which "1" means "very dissatisfied" and "10" means "very satisfied," how satisfied are you with the Agency's services?
Confirmation of Expectations	Considering all of your expectations, to what extent has the Agency fallen short of your expectations or exceeded your expectations? Using a 10 point scale on which "1" means "falls short of your expectations" and "10" means "exceeds your expectations," to what extent has the Agency fallen short of or exceeded your expectations?
Comparison to an Ideal	Forget the Agency for a moment. Now, I want you to imagine an ideal agency that offers the same types of services. How well do you think the Agency compares with that ideal agency? Please use a 10 point scale on which "1" means "not very close to the ideal," and "10" means "very close to the ideal."
Confidence	How confident are you that the Agency will do a good job providing the services that you used in the future? Using a 10 point scale on which "1" means "not at all confident" and "10" means "very confident," how confident are you that the Agency will do a good job in the future?
Word-of-Mouth	If asked, how willing would you be to say positive things about the job the Agency is doing in administering the kinds of services you experienced? Using a 10 point scale on which "1" means "not at all willing" and 10 means "very willing," how willing would you be to say positive things about the Agency?

as our satisfaction questions, above; recalling one of these sample drivers, measuring "information delivery" might mean measuring all of the completeness, quality, timeliness, clarity, and accessibility of the agency's information. But because, for reasons just mentioned, attempting to measure each of these aspects of information delivery in a single question would lead to difficulties for both the respondent and the researcher, one can choose to measure either only one of these aspects of information delivery as definitive of the entire user experience, which is likely to provide an incomplete picture at best, or measure several aspects in separate survey questions and model them together in some fashion during analysis. While the practical implications of asking several questions related to one another and modeling them jointly during analysis may be unclear at this point, we provide more detail on this type of multiple-item or *latent variable* measurement in the next chapter.

Fourth, along with those few short, concise questions deemed most important to include in a questionnaire, it is also useful to add demographic questions to a survey, questions asking the respondent to identify their age, gender, race, location, and income, along with related information.[17] In the first instance, demographic questions are useful for cross-checking the sample of data collected, and to ensure that the sample "looks like" the population being investigated. If, for example, you receive data collected using your questionnaire that consists of 75 percent male respondents, when you know the underlying population to be roughly equally split between men and women, you can safely conclude that your sample may not be representative, and thus any conclusions you draw from the data may not be reliable. Moreover, demographic questions permit the analyst to segment the data once collected and to compare satisfaction and results from other variables across subgroups (men versus women, old versus young). In turn, the ability to split and compare the data in this way can help the researcher differentiate satisfaction among different groups of users, and it is often the case that some groups are more or less satisfied than others (a phenomenon we discuss in a later chapter).

Again, while this brief review is far from a comprehensive look at questionnaire design, these core issues will certainly need to be addressed when devising a citizen satisfaction survey.

Data Collection and Sample Size

Much like the subject of questionnaire design, how best to collect data using a survey, and the appropriate amount of data to collect (i.e., the number of completed interviews of citizen/respondents), are topics worthy of entire volumes.[18] Furthermore, with the relatively recent introduction of new communications technologies used to conduct interviewing, these questions have become even more complex; choosing between landline telephone interviewing, online interviewing, and wireless telephone interviewing, along with traditional methods such as face-to-face interviewing or interviewing by mailed forms, is an issue that challenges every researcher. But once again, a few rules of thumb are worth noting, and in this case the matter can be reduced to an essential tension between two values: the collection of reliable data and controlling data collection costs.

Perhaps the single most important goal when collecting survey data is to collect a *representative random sample.* That is, assuming that we have neither the money, the time, nor the inclination to interview every single citizen that has experienced a government agency, we are left with the option of identifying a sample of the overall population, interviewing that sample, and basing our analysis and conclusions on the insights gleaned from that sample. While the final dataset may contain only a small fraction of the total population that could have responded to a survey, if the sample "looks like" the overall population (is representative of it) and if every member of the population had a theoretically equal chance of being selected for interviewing (random selection), then statisticians are comfortable making inferences and drawing conclusions about the whole population based on a sample.[19] Paying significant attention to the collection of a sample and that sample's randomness and representativeness is, therefore, of the utmost importance when embarking on a satisfaction measurement program, or for that matter, any survey research project.

Yet for nearly every research project involving the collection of data using a survey, data collection is the single most expensive aspect of the project. For large projects involving the interviewing of tens of thousands of respondents, data collection alone can run into the hundreds-of-thousands of dollars, and sometimes more. For projects where the population or group of eligible potential respondents is small or very difficult to reach, the costs (or "cost per interview" [CPI], as it is called in the market research business) can skyrocket even higher. But attempting to reduce these costs by collecting a very small amount of data (just a few interviews) or using questionable methods to collect it (such as the "comment card" handed to you by a waiter or waitress who proceeds to stand over you glaring at your answers as you complete it, introducing enormous bias into the study) often leads to unreliable results that can in turn lead to incorrect inferences and conclusions.

The real challenge for the survey researcher, then, is to balance these two realities, to find a cost-effective data collection method that results in a representative random sample that contains as little bias as possible. For most survey research projects operating today, two of the data collection methods mentioned above—telephone interviewing (either landline or wireless) and online interviewing—are typically preferred. These two methods are described below.

1. *Random-Digit-Dial Telephone Interviewing*: Random-digit-dial (or RDD) telephone interviewing draws a random sample of telephone numbers proportional to the population density of various geographic regions (in the United States, this is usually based on the population within telephone area codes). The selected or sampled phone numbers are then called at random for interviewing. Interviewing is done over the telephone, and is usually conducted by a market research firm and/or other trained interview technicians, often using computer-assisted telephone interviewing, or CATI, which displays the questions in a particular order on a computer terminal for the interviewer to read and input responses. All other things being equal, RDD is probably the best method in terms of identifying and interviewing a representative sample of citizens, but it is also one of the more expensive data collection methods. Furthermore, the proliferation of "cell phone–only" households and number portability (which may mean that area codes no longer matter in terms of actual geographic distribution) has diminished confidence among researchers that this method provides a sample as representative of the general population as it did in the past.

2. *Online/Internet Interviewing*: Many survey researchers are now attempting to transition at least some data collection to the Internet, as this collection method tends to be far less expensive. Furthermore, many researchers are becoming more confident that the Internet-using population has grown to approximate the general population. Using this method, invitations to participate in the survey are sent via email to a potential respondent (often identified via a panel of email addresses), and the interview itself is completed over the Internet, typically using an interactive form and a web server. While far less expensive, two problems that can accompany this type of data collection are a violation of the principles of randomness and representativeness mentioned above, as the Internet may not be perfectly representative of the overall population (or at least as representative as telephones), and difficulties associated with identifying potential respondents via email. Yet neither of these concerns are as troubling for government agencies, as many of these agencies have extensive information about the citizen-users they are interested in interviewing (more so than most private sector firms, for instance), including their names and email addresses, and therefore this method can often be confidently implemented in this context.

Turning now to the size of the sample, or the number of interviews, that should be collected when embarking on a satisfaction measurement project. And here too, when deciding how many interviews to collect, the decision ultimately revolves around a balance between reliable results and data collection costs.

All other things being equal, researchers would almost always prefer to have access to more data rather than less. If given a choice between two samples, one comprised of 250 interviews and the other 500 interviews, and both collected according to the principles of randomness and representativeness mentioned earlier, the latter should always be our preference. But unfortunately, collecting data is not free. In practical terms, this means that adding enough additional data to a sample to positively impact our "confidence" in that sample, usually measured by way of a confidence interval (CI), can quickly become very expensive. But even assuming a huge amount of money

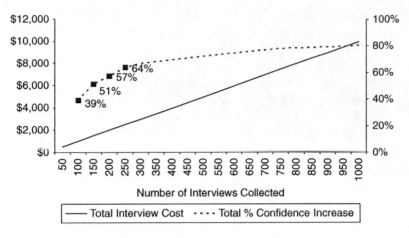

Figure 3.1 The diminishing returns of data collection.

at our disposal with which to collect data, it still makes little sense to do so past a certain point. This is because the gains we get in terms of improved precision (i.e., a decrease in the size of our CI) are not constant, while data collection costs (i.e., CPI) typically are. Figure 3.1 shows an example—using the changing standard deviations, standard errors and CIs underlying a variable—of the relationship between gains in confidence in a sample as sample size increases and dollars spent, and the diminishing returns in confidence as the amount of collected data grows.

The graph begins with a very small sample, including only 50 completed interviews, and shows that the improvements in confidence in our data (marked by a total percentage decrease in the CI) are rapid and significant as the sample grows. If we start with a sample of only 50 interviews, the CI would be large, and a large CI will give us little confidence in the reliability of our results. If we double the sample to 100 cases, our CI improves 39 percent (is 39% smaller), providing a much narrower "confidence band" and giving us far more faith in our results. With the addition of another 50 interviews for a total of 150, our CI drops considerably again, for a total improvement of 51 percent. Add another 50 cases up to 200 total interviews, and the overall improvement is 57 percent, with a total improvement of 64 percent at a sample size of 250. At each step in the chart we have added 50 additional interviews, with each interview costing the same amount. So our final sample of 1000 interviews costs $10,000 (i.e., assuming a constant CPI of $10, which is actually relatively inexpensive), or 1900 percent more than our original sample of 50. As a consequence, our CI has improved considerably, but the total improvement in confidence at 1000 cases is only 80 percent. And most of that improvement occurred early along as we first added more sample; most of those gains in confidence or precision (64%) were achieved by increasing the sample from 50 to 250 interviews.

What this example shows is that collecting more data is one way to increase your confidence in your satisfaction score and overall results, but after a certain point this is not an efficient option. Data collection is expensive, and eventually we receive very little return in the way of more precision for our investment. For most citizen satisfaction measures, therefore, and again using experience as a guide, a sample of 250 to 1000 cases (or total interviews) is usually sufficient, at least when measuring a single government program or agency and producing a single satisfaction score. If interested in producing satisfaction results for several contact points within a program, several programs within an agency, or several agencies within a department, additional data collection may be advisable.

Conclusion

In this chapter we have provided a primer aimed at a better understanding of some key steps and considerations involved in citizen satisfaction measurement, beginning with decisions about what (a citizen-facing program or agency) and who (citizens with actual contact and experience with the agency) to measure, the variables to include in the questionnaire alongside satisfaction (drivers of satisfaction, satisfaction itself, and its outcomes), how to operationalize satisfaction, how to design a questionnaire, and how to sample and interview using that questionnaire. In the next chapter we continue this discussion, moving on to consider some statistical methods for analyzing the data once it is collected in a way that maximizes our ability to both identify areas in need of improvement, and outcomes of satisfaction that governments often seek.

CHAPTER 4

The Practice of Citizen Satisfaction Measurement: Statistical Analysis and Modeling

Introduction

In the last chapter, we reviewed a number of important steps in a citizen satisfaction measurement project: agency and population-of-measurement selection, the identification of drivers and outcomes to measure within a survey alongside the satisfaction concept, various perspectives on how the satisfaction concept can be operationalized, questionnaire design, interviewing methods, and sample size considerations. In this chapter, we proceed by considering some of the statistical methods that can be used to examine the data collected through a satisfaction survey. While statistical methods for examining survey data are numerous and vary widely, and while researchers often have their own preferred set of methods (and sometimes cling to these methods passionately), here we will suggest that the type of statistical analysis we ultimately recommend—a multiple-item measure, latent variable, structural equation modeling approach (sometimes also called a "path modeling" approach)—is one often-used and well-tested technique for generating valid, reliable satisfaction scores and for dynamically relating satisfaction to its key influencing factors and its outcomes. In turn, this kind of data analysis can offer useful, accurate, and actionable insights into the practical reforms government agencies can make toward improving citizen satisfaction, as well as related outcomes like citizen trust.

Data Analysis and Statistical Modeling

When all of the steps outlined in the last chapter have been completed, and a sample of survey responses has been collected from a population using a satisfaction questionnaire eliciting respondents' perceptions concerning their experiences with a government agency (or program, or service), we have then arrived at the final stage of the measurement process, the last step prior to the interpretation of results and implementation of practical reforms aimed at addressing recognized deficiencies and improving satisfaction (a set of processes we will consider in chapter 5). We are ready, that is, to model and statistically analyze our data. While there are as many ways to analyze any dataset as there are researchers and statisticians, here we will ultimately examine one popular set of methods used increasingly by academics and other researchers as a preferred, well-tested approach for doing so—structural equation modeling (SEM). These methods are designed specifically for the analysis of complex datasets with a large number of interrelated variables and many underlying relationships between the variables, and can ultimately provide the researcher with significant practical insights when interpreting results. For these reasons, this set of methods has proven useful to many researchers (and government agencies) seeking strategies for improving their relationships with their citizen-users over the last few decades.

But before we outline SEM methods in some detail, it is worthwhile to first pause and—after describing the data that we will analyze in this chapter and the next—consider some alternative statistical techniques that can be, and often are, employed when analyzing citizen satisfaction and related data. A brief review of these methods will help show both their legitimate applications and enduring usefulness as stages in the analysis of this type of data (or any dataset, for that matter), and thus the reasons for their enduring popularity among researchers, as well as some of the drawbacks that make these methods of limited usefulness.

One final note: While we will by necessity be dealing with some moderately complex statistical techniques throughout this chapter, we will attempt to keep our discussions as simple and "stripped-down" as possible, so that readers at all levels of technical expertise will (hopefully) be able to follow along. The unavoidable drawback of this approach is that we risk oversimplifying some fairly involved, detail-oriented methods and processes, as well as the oftentimes complex software packages used to implements these methods and processes. Yet by adopting this approach, those already familiar with the methods will need no additional explanation, and those unfamiliar won't be burdened with excessive technical detail that is not of immediate interest (or even vaguely comprehensible). Nevertheless, throughout this chapter and in the references at the end of the chapter, some additional resources and citations are offered to provide the reader with opportunities for investigating these techniques more thoroughly, if so desired. Moreover, the appendix at the end of the text provides some additional output and analysis that is typically included in this kind of analysis, but omitted from this chapter.

Dataset Description

The data we analyze below, in chapter 5, and in parts of chapter 6 come from the ACSI, a research project that has collected survey data regarding consumer satisfaction across the public and private sectors for nearly two decades, and a project that was outlined in some detail in the "Introduction." More specifically, the dataset we analyze here consists of interviews of respondents who have actually experienced a US federal government program, agency or department and its services in the prior year, a fact established through a screening question like that outlined in chapter 3. Measured through a questionnaire asking survey items like those also outlined earlier (including all of the questions defined there, in addition to many others), the dataset is a pooled, multiyear sample collected between 2007 and 2011, and containing a total of more than 7,200 interviews of citizens (N=7204).[1] All told, across all five years of data collection, the citizens responding experienced nearly 60 distinct federal government programs, agencies and departments, meaning that the sample reflects (at least to some extent) citizen perceptions with a large proportion of the federal government and its services, rather than just a single agency or program. It is this sample of data that we will analyze in all of the exercises below, and while this diverse sample might not serve to draw conclusions about any one particular government service or program—at least in this highly aggregated form—it will prove more than adequate for illustrating the statistical methods we wish to consider.

Mean Score Descriptive Statistics, Analysis, and Benchmarking

One of the most basic tasks of any researcher or data analyst is to carefully examine new data when it is first received, once interviewing and data collection using a questionnaire is complete, and the collected data is organized into some type of workable, analyzable spreadsheet. In its "raw" form, prior to any kind of processing or analysis, survey data is just some collection of columns (representing individual measured variables) and rows (representing individual cases, or individual respondent interviews) inserted into a spreadsheet or matrix, complete with cells populated with numbers reflecting each respondent's answer to each question in the survey. Alone, without any additional analysis, these numbers tell us virtually nothing about the data collected, or about the citizens who have answered the questionnaire and their perceptions of the government agency or program they have experienced. And so the first thing virtually every researcher does after receiving new data is to generate *descriptive statistics*, typically including mean scores (arithmetic averages), the number of valid responses (or number of interviews, typically called the sample's total "N"), the range of scores from low to high, the standard deviation, and so forth, for each of the variables (or at least all of the substantive variables that are to be analyzed) included in the dataset, with the goal of seeing what the collected data actually "looks like."

Once generated, these descriptive statistics will usually be presented in a table similar to table 4.1, which includes results for several substantive variables in the sample, including a satisfaction variable, variables reflecting factors that might be thought to influence satisfaction, and outcomes of satisfaction:

In table 4.1, we see ordinary descriptive statistics for a cohort of variables very much like those one might find in a citizen satisfaction dataset. More specifically, this table includes results from ten variables in all, including survey items measuring the respondents' overall satisfaction with the federal government agency experienced,

Table 4.1 Sample descriptive statistics for citizen satisfaction questionnaire variables

Variable	N	MIN	MAX	MEAN	SD
Overall Satisfaction	7204	1	10	7.54	2.47
Overall Expectations	7120	1	10	7.12	2.45
Ease of Info	7114	1	10	7.64	2.49
Clarity of Info	7177	1	10	7.56	2.46
Timeliness of Process	7137	1	10	7.48	2.74
Ease of Process	7075	1	10	7.44	2.71
Courtesy of Personnel	2826	1	10	8.15	2.46
Professionalism of Personnel	2831	1	10	8.21	2.37
Confidence in Agency	7144	1	10	7.09	2.70
Trust in Government (Overall)	5628	1	10	4.46	2.54

his or her prior expectations about their experiences with the agency, the ease of receiving information and the clarity of the information received, the timeliness (efficiency) and ease of the process experienced, the courtesy and professionalism of the personnel interacted with, the respondent's confidence in the particular agency experienced, and the respondent's trust in the government in Washington, DC overall. (Question wording for several of these variables can be found in the sample questions provided in chapter 3.)

Under each column and to the right of each variable is basic information about that variable. In descriptive statistics analysis, analysis will generally include several statistics, many of which are included here: the total number of valid cases or interview responses for each variable (the "N"),[2] the low and high score (or range) for each variable ("MIN" and "MAX"), the arithmetic average or mean score for all of the respondents that responded regarding the variable ("MEAN"), and the standard deviation (a measure of sample variance around the mean score) for each variable ("SD").

In the first instance, as mentioned earlier, researchers will almost always first examine these descriptive statistics in order to get a better feel for the data they will be working with, and to examine the "cleanliness" and accuracy of that data prior to any additional, more complex analyses. Within this process, statisticians will normally ask questions like: Are more cases missing than was anticipated, possibly indicating errors in the data collection process? Do any of the variables have low or high scores outside the anticipated range, possibly indicating errors (such as data cleaning or coding errors) in the data itself? Are the mean scores lower or higher than expected for some particular variable? Do any of the variables show a much larger standard deviation than the others, perhaps indicating a set of responses significantly deviating from a normal distribution (or at least exhibiting a more skewed distribution than the other variables, which can certainly impact results and interpretation)? Answers to these and similar questions are vital before proceeding to more complex kinds of analyses, as they increase confidence that this analysis will be error-free and reliable.

Yet some researchers will rely mostly or even entirely on the analysis of descriptive statistics, and draw vital conclusions about the data (and the respondents who provided the data) from these alone. Looking exclusively at these numbers—and imagining for a moment, just for the purposes of this exercise, that the results represent data for a just a single, particular government agency or program we are focused on improving—and there are certainly conclusions we might want to draw about citizens' experiences with the hypothetical agency from this data. For example, the variables measuring courteousness and professionalism of customer service personnel both score quite well relative to the other variables, and while we will not report the technical details here, formal tests of statistical significance (two-tailed "t-tests," in this instance) confirm that these variables score statistically significantly higher than all of the other identified drivers (or influencing factors) of citizen satisfaction (such as prior expectations, ease of accessing information, clarity of information, etc.).[3] So while citizens may not look favorably at all aspects of their encounters with this government agency, they do report being treated with courtesy and professionalism by agency staff, a positive result for the government agency, and perhaps a justification for identifying this aspect of government services as best-in-class.

Furthermore, it is possible to go even a bit further in interpreting these results. With a mean of 7.54, the overall satisfaction score registers significantly higher than the overall expectations score (7.12), which suggests that while citizens have relatively low prior expectations about what they will experience from the government, the actual experience (in terms of satisfaction) significantly exceeds these expectations. A persistent finding across US federal government agencies (and one that we discuss in more detail in chapter 6), this result suggests that citizens' expectations are depressed relative to what they report actually receiving, a result that likely speaks to negative forces impacting citizens' views of the federal government prior to their experiences. Furthermore, while both of the trust variables score relatively poorly, the mean for confidence in the agency (7.09) dramatically exceeds the score for trust in the government overall (4.46), indicating that citizens experiencing this agency have more confidence in that agency than they trust the government in Washington, DC as a whole, another common finding.

The simple interpretive exercises described above show how even just basic descriptive statistics from a single (hypothetical) agency sample of data can provide information sufficient to draw at least some conclusions about how a government agency and its services are performing, and the perceptions of the respondents experiencing the agency. Moreover, with access to two (or multiple) datasets covering more than one government agency that include an identical set of variables, we would be able to use these descriptive statistics to begin the type of performance benchmarking described earlier, with the goal of identifying agencies that provide their citizens strong, positive experiences along one or multiple dimensions. That is, with statistics for several agencies at our disposal and the ability to compare and benchmark scores, and thus to identify which agency or agencies are outperforming others, we are well on our way to identifying best practices that can guide reform efforts across government agencies. And in the next chapter, we provide multiple examples of this kind of competitive benchmarking of satisfaction data within a "priority matrix" toward drawing conclusions about best practices.

Yet all of these legitimate and important uses for descriptive statistics notwithstanding, these methods are certainly not a panacea. While these techniques can provide a type of first-order information for understanding how well one or several agencies are performing in terms of satisfaction and along other dimensions, and might also provide information for beginning the process of performance benchmarking and best practice identification, there are significant limitations to their usefulness. Most importantly, this analysis tells us virtually nothing about the factors or variables that are *most influential in driving citizen satisfaction.* In other words, while we can use these results to say which variables are doing better or worse (in an absolute, mean-score-level sense) and how satisfied citizens are, we cannot concretely and accurately determine which one or few factors (such as professionalism, courtesy, information, etc.) are most responsible for driving satisfaction or trust higher or lower, and thus how to strategically optimize satisfaction through improvements in other areas. To draw these kinds of conclusions, more advanced statistical methods are required.

Bivariate Correlation Analysis and Multiple Linear Regression

Beyond the basic descriptive statistics approach, and given the just-outlined weaknesses of this approach, there are many additional, only slightly more complicated statistical tools that researchers rely on when analyzing survey data. One such approach is bivariate correlation analysis, through which the strength of the relationship (or interrelationship, or "co"-relationship) between pairs of individual variables can be determined. Using the same data described earlier through which descriptive statistics were produced, now consider the correlations presented in table 4.2.

In the simplest terms, what these correlations show (which represent, more technically, "Pearson's product-moment correlation coefficients") is the strength of the relationship between any two variables in our dataset, or the amount the two variables tend to move together up and down within the sample of data. A larger correlation closer to "1.0" is indicative of a stronger positive relationship, with the two variables moving together increasingly closely (i.e., as one variable increases, the other tends to do so as well and at a similar magnitude as the correlation approaches 1.0); a correlation close to "0.0" indicates little or no relationship, or joint movement, between the variables; and a correlation closer to "−1.0" is indicative of an inverse or negative relationship, where as one variable moves higher, the other tends to move lower at a similar magnitude.

So for instance, starting with the "Overall Sat." (Overall Satisfaction) variable in the first row of the farthest left-hand column, we can see (working across the row to the right) that satisfaction has a

Table 4.2 Bivariate correlations for citizen satisfaction questionnaire variables

	Overall Sat.	Overall Exp.	Ease of Info	Clarity of Info	Time. of Process	Ease of Process	Court. of Personnel	Prof. of Personnel	Conf. in Agency	Trust in Govt. (Overall)
Overall Sat.	1	0.517	0.638	0.656	0.725	0.745	0.658	0.685	0.772	0.313
Overall Exp.	0.517	1	0.452	0.453	0.431	0.440	0.356	0.389	0.505	0.266
Ease of Info	0.638	0.452	1	0.733	0.660	0.699	0.551	0.565	0.580	0.238
Clarity of Info	0.656	0.453	0.733	1	0.648	0.665	0.579	0.590	0.614	0.267
Time. of Process	0.725	0.431	0.660	0.648	1	0.811	0.620	0.627	0.653	0.278
Ease of Process	0.745	0.440	0.699	0.665	0.811	1	0.638	0.640	0.664	0.277
Court. of Personnel	0.658	0.356	0.551	0.579	0.620	0.638	1	0.872	0.610	0.225
Prof. of Personnel	0.685	0.389	0.565	0.590	0.627	0.640	0.872	1	0.639	0.237
Conf. in Agency	0.772	0.505	0.580	0.614	0.653	0.664	0.610	0.639	1	0.379
Trust in Govt (Overall)	0.313	0.266	0.238	0.267	0.278	0.277	0.225	0.237	0.379	1

Note: All correlations significant at the $p < 0.05$ level.

fairly strong relationship with "Overall Exp." (Overall Expectations) of 0.517, a slightly higher correlation with "Ease of Info" (0.638), but an even stronger relationship of 0.745 with "Ease of Process" among the influencing factors or drivers of satisfaction included in the dataset.[4] Likewise, focusing now on outcomes of satisfaction like trust, we see that Overall Sat. has a strong correlation with "Conf. in Agency" (Agency Confidence) of 0.772, but a smaller correlation with "Trust in Govt." (Trust in the Government Overall) of 0.313.

In practical terms, what these correlations tell us is, based on this particular sample of data, how one variable is likely to move were another variable to move as well, and vice versa. This means, for instance, that an increase in "Ease of Process" is likely (or at minimum, so it is suggested within this data at this moment in time) to coincide with a larger increase in "Overall Sat." than the same identical increase in either "Overall Exp." or "Ease of Info.," that these two variables are more strongly related and more codependent upon one another. Similarly, these correlations indicate that as "Overall Sat." increases, "Conf. in Agency" is likely to increase more than "Trust in Govt.," all other things being equal.[5]

In essence, correlation analysis can help us begin to answer some of the lingering questions descriptive statistics analysis, as outlined earlier, cannot. Most importantly, as shown in these brief examples, correlation analysis is able to tell us which variables are most strongly related to one another. As such, a researcher might use these correlations to determine the variable that is *most strongly related to citizen satisfaction*, and in this way get a better understanding of which of these identified drivers of satisfaction to focus on in working to improve citizen satisfaction with the agency, as well as how increases in satisfaction are likely to influence outcomes like confidence in an agency and trust in the government overall. That is, if we know which of these factors tends to move in tandem with satisfaction most strongly, we might gain some insights into the activities that, if improvements were to be made there, *might result in the biggest satisfaction increase*. In this way, these correlations might be (and sometimes are) used to help us identify (or at least begin the process of identifying) candidate areas for focusing our practical improvement efforts and reform strategies, discovering those areas that are most likely to yield the largest improvement in satisfaction if they themselves are improved.

But in this case too, correlation analysis should not be seen as an ultimate solution, as this technique also has significant limitations. While correlations can tell us about the strength of the relationship between many individual pairs of variables in our dataset, they do so only in isolation. What they cannot reveal, on the other hand, are the relationships between multiple, interrelated variables that interact with one another and also have a joint impact on an outcome (or dependent) variable like citizen satisfaction, and which of the factors is *relatively more important in driving satisfaction*. And it is precisely this kind of "real-world" technique that is often needed to adequately analyze citizen satisfaction data, given that under most circumstances it is reasonable and/or necessary to assume that multiple factors (as opposed to just one factor) are influencing satisfaction with an experience with a government agency simultaneously, that these factors are also correlated with one another, and that some may be more powerful drivers of satisfaction than others. A common method for understanding these more complex relationships, one that explicitly recognizes that many factors tend to influence a dependent variable like citizen satisfaction simultaneously and that these variables themselves are interdependent, is multiple linear regression (MLR).

While relying on the same basic family of statistical techniques, multiple linear regression is generally viewed as a step above bivariate correlation analysis, so to speak, in its complexity and rigor, and it allows the researcher to address the primary limitations of correlation analysis mentioned earlier.[6] Simply put, and unlike correlation analysis, MLR allows us to simultaneously estimate the relationship between several independent variables (or influencing factors) and one dependent variable (or outcome, or influenced factor), like citizen satisfaction. Again using the same data as earlier, table 4.3 includes most of the typical output one would produce and display when employing multiple linear regression methods to analyze data:

In this MLR model, overall satisfaction ("Overall Sat.," while not explicitly listed anywhere) has been defined as our dependent variable, the variable we are interested in understanding and explaining

Table 4.3 Multiple linear regression results

	Unstandardized Estimate	Standard Error	Standardized Estimate	t	p
Constant	0.014	0.114		0.126	0.900
Overall Expectations	0.129	0.013	0.125	10.138	0.000
Ease of Info	0.017	0.018	0.017	0.974	0.330
Clarity of Info	0.135	0.018	0.131	7.547	0.000
Timeliness of Process	0.238	0.018	0.271	13.410	0.000
Ease of Process	0.198	0.019	0.221	10.563	0.000
Courtesy of Personnel	0.042	0.024	0.039	1.753	0.080
Professionalism of Personnel	0.231	0.025	0.205	9.162	0.000
R^2	0.704				
Adjusted R^2	0.703				

the variability in (or the movement up and down). The seven variables in the left-hand column—from overall expectations at the top, to professionalism of personnel at the bottom—have been defined as independent or predictor variables in the model. In other words, in this model we are suggesting (we expect and/or have formally hypothesized) that these seven variables are likely to have significant effects on satisfaction as they move up and down in value, that these are "significant predictors" of citizen satisfaction. And through this exercise, our most important goal is to find the one or few variables that have the largest significant effect on satisfaction, those areas where practical improvement efforts might be focused in order to realize the greatest positive change in satisfaction. The output in the first row, labeled "Constant" and sometimes also called an "intercept," helps determine the expected average value of "Overall Sat." when all of the other independent variables are held constant at "0," and isn't of particular concern for our purposes here.

Much like the correlation coefficients discussed earlier, the main output from MLR analyses are the regression coefficients (labeled "Unstandardized Estimate" in the table), which indicate how much citizen satisfaction changes assuming a 1-point increase in the independent variable, and *holding all of the other influencing factors (or independent variables) constant*. In other words, these regression coefficients tell us the effect of each independent variable on citizen satisfaction while also assuming the existence of (but *controlling* for) these other potentially important predictors of satisfaction, and this is precisely what allows us to better understand the joint effect of several variables on citizen satisfaction than we can using simple bivariate correlations, to model our data in a more complex, realistic way.

Looking at the remaining output, the "Standard Error" tells us the variance of the coefficient of each independent variable on the dependent variable; the "Standardized Estimates" are the effect of each independent variable on the dependent after adjusting for each variables' variance; the "t" and "p" values are common measures of statistical significance, estimates of how likely the effect of the independent variable is real and not just the result of random chance (a p-value closer to "0.000" indicates a smaller probability of random chance having produced the relationship); and the "R^2" and "Adjusted R^2" are measures of model goodness-of-fit, telling us the amount of the variance in the dependent variable we have successfully explained, with a number closer to 1.00 better because indicative of a larger amount of explained variance.

Based on the output provided above and this brief overview of MLR techniques, we can now draw some conclusions about our data, and more importantly, start to determine those areas most influential over citizen satisfaction, and thus those areas we may want to focus improvement efforts on in order to improve satisfaction. Looking at the coefficients in the "Unstandardized Estimate" column, we see that three variables standout in the size of their effect on satisfaction: "Timeliness of Process," "Ease of Process," and "Professionalism of Personnel."[7] With coefficients ranging from 0.198 to 0.238 (again, indicating the predicted change in citizen satisfaction should the independent variable increase by 1-point on the 1–10 scale), each of these variables has a large and highly significant (as confirmed by the p-values of 0.000 for each) effect on citizen satisfaction, larger than the other variables included in the analysis.

Two of the other variables included in the model ("Overall Expectations" and "Clarity of Info.") have significant effects on satisfaction as well, but the coefficients are smaller. Thus while we shouldn't interpret these variables (or the activities they are related to) as entirely irrelevant, they are not found to have the largest effects on satisfaction. Finally, two variables, "Ease of Info." and "Courtesy of Personnel" have much smaller and statistically insignificant effects on satisfaction, a conclusion we would draw based on the p-values greater than 0.05 (and the somewhat arbitrary convention of treating any p-value above 0.05 as non-significant). These results would usually be interpreted as evidence that the relationship between these variables and "Overall Sat." is not large enough to deem "real," or larger than what we would expect to see from random chance alone. In sum, based on these MLR results and statistics, we would conclude that three features—"Timeliness of Process," "Ease of Process," and "Professionalism of Personnel"—are most influential in driving citizen satisfaction higher and lower, and thus from a practical perspective, focusing agency reform efforts on these areas might be the best strategy for realizing improvements in satisfaction.

While an undeniably useful and effective technique, and indeed, the bedrock method underpinning much of the statistical analysis used by researchers today and over the past century, the main problems with MLR are its somewhat restrictive, inflexible modeling requirements. While MLR allows one to include multiple independent variables as predictors of a dependent variable during analysis, which at least better approximates real-world conditions, the method does not allow for the analysis of more complex relationships. This is particularly problematic in terms of satisfaction analysis, as it is typically viewed as an "unobservable" concept that does not lend itself to direct observation or measurement; in other words, no single question or variable is likely to be particularly successful in realizing a "true" estimate of satisfaction, but will only provide a partial view of it, as we mentioned in the last chapter. As such, researchers often attempt to come closer to a complete estimate of satisfaction by measuring multiple questions (or variables) in a survey that tap into satisfaction's different dimensions. The same can be said for many of the variables considered above; ease and timeliness of a process, as well as courtesy and professionalism, could be argued to reflect underlying dimensions of a single unobservable phenomenon (a "process" and "customer service," respectively).[8]

What is more, when designing a model researchers often want to consider the relationship between satisfaction, its influencing factors and its outcomes (variables like trust, confidence, and complaints) simultaneously, as part a more complex, interrelated and dynamic *system of relationships* connected together, rather than as a simple relationship or a series of single-equation models. However, as a method MLR is incapable of either including multiple dependent variables in a single model or in estimating more complex multiple-equation (or structural) relationships, leading researchers to often turn to alternative statistical techniques that better accommodate these situations. One such technique is SEM, the method that we describe next.

SEM of Satisfaction Data

Having now briefly examined a few commonplace methods for analyzing satisfaction survey data, and having discussed both the benefits and some of the weaknesses of these methods, we turn to an analysis of one preferred method for investigating this type of data, the method that, we will argue, provides the most benefit in reaching conclusions and identifying improvements that will in turn enhance both citizen satisfaction and outcomes of satisfaction: structural equation modeling or SEM.

Before beginning this discussion in earnest, it must first be noted that SEM is not considered a particularly easy-to-apply technique. Even among competent researchers and analysts, SEM is sometimes viewed as an esoteric, difficult method requiring the participation of an expert statistician steeped in these techniques. Whether this perception is accurate or not (and in some cases, researchers tend to overstate the method's complexity), in what follows we will attempt to focus on the core output of satisfaction survey data analyzed using SEM, rather than the nitty-gritty technical detail underlying these methods. In the end, a clear understanding of the practical benefits of data analyzed using these methods is more important than precisely how the results are computed, at least for our purposes in this text, and so here is where we will focus. (And as noted earlier, the appendix at the end of the book includes some additional output and discussion regarding Partial Least Squares path modeling (PLS-PM), the specific type of SEM we employ here.)

As a novel statistical technique, SEM has a relatively long and colorful history, beginning with applications in the early 1920s from evolutionary biology and genetics, disciplines that often require the study of multiple dependent variables explained by a potentially huge number of explanatory factors or independent variables. While it is unnecessary to review the entire history of the method here,[9] suffice it to say that SEM—originally known as "path analysis," and later (and sometimes still) referred to as "causal modeling"—is a technique that allows for a large number of variables to be modeled together in a system of equations guided by both theory and an attempt to best approximate and understand complex, real-world relationships. Today this family of methods is one of the more popular among social scientists analyzing data across a variety of academic disciplines. Likewise, this method has grown increasingly popular among both academic researchers and research practitioners analyzing government performance data, and especially citizen satisfaction data.[10]

At its core, SEM is little more than an advancement on and extension of both correlation analysis and the MLR methods outlined above, a "third generation" statistical technique for understanding the relationships between variables. But unlike ordinary multiple regression analysis, which only allows the researcher to examine the effect of a single group of independent variables on a single dependent variable (with all variables required to meet fairly rigid criteria), SEM permits the simultaneous modeling of multiple sets of highly correlated independent variables (multiple equations) on multiple dependent variables in a series of interrelationships. SEM techniques also allow the researcher to model several individual survey questions together as elements within a broader phenomenon or concept, and to create what are known as latent variables (or alternatively, "unobservable variables," "constructs," or "composite variables"). And as mentioned earlier, or at least alluded to in the review of alternative methods provided, it is often the case that variables used in satisfaction surveys are best modeled together and considered as parts of broader conceptual phenomena.

Much like the alternative methods discussed earlier, results obtained through SEM contain many different pieces of output, most of which would be of only passing and technical interest, such as latent variable and overall model goodness-of-fit statistics, variable loadings and cross-loadings, tests of convergent and discriminant validity, and so on (see the appendix for some of this output and a discussion of it). But most importantly for our purposes, the output includes two pieces of information that we have already discussed to some extent and that should be gleaned from the data collected via any and every citizen satisfaction survey, the two pieces of information that drive many of the objectives underpinning this type of measurement for government.

The first piece of information is a metric of performance in an absolute sense, which can be measured as a mean score for the measured variables across all of the respondents interviewed and included in the sample, like the arithmetic averages produced in ordinary descriptive statistics and discussed earlier in this chapter. That is, data generated from responses to satisfaction survey questions, with respondents rating their satisfaction and trust, or some other aspect of their experience with an agency, if looked at as an average of all of these responses, can be regarded as the *level of performance* for the agency for an activity. And as shown earlier, neither SEM nor any more complicated statistical technique beside basic descriptive statistics analysis are needed to produce these scores, at least in some form.

The primary difference between SEM and other statistical methods is how these mean scores are calculated. The type of single-question mean scores we examined earlier when reviewing basic descriptive statistics are, of course, the most common type of mean that can be computed. But an alternative—and, in the eyes of many, superior—type of mean score can be produced through SEM techniques. Put simply, because SEM relies on latent variables composed of multiple individual survey questions, mean scores can be produced that reflect a *weighted average of several individual questions included in a latent variable*. In turn, these weighted latent variable mean scores offer ratings of performance for overall conceptual phenomena (rather than just specific aspects of phenomena measured through single survey items) that are highly useful for understanding and comparing government performance on satisfaction or some other attribute in a more complex environment, while also sometimes proving superior in terms of statistical validity and reliability.[11]

But as we discussed earlier, it is rarely sufficient to know only the level of performance on one or some set of variables, at least so long as practical improvements and reforms remain a central objective of an agency's satisfaction measurement program. Again, this is precisely the reason researchers turn to MLR or a technique like SEM to develop a better understanding of the relationships in their data. And the impacts or effects provided through SEM (sometimes also called "path coefficients" or "effects") are generally considered superior to those produced in MLR, precisely because they are estimated as part of a system of relationships with more complex latent variables that more accurately reflect real-world conditions and the multiple interdependencies contained therein. These SEM coefficients, therefore, become the second piece of the analytical puzzle gleaned from satisfaction survey data using this method, the links between the activities defined as the predicting latent variables, citizen satisfaction, and outcomes of satisfaction that help guide the researcher towards identifying those areas that might provide the greatest leverage in improving satisfaction, a topic we expand on below.

One final beneficial feature of SEM is that the relationships between the manifest and latent variables and between the latent variables themselves included in the model are usually displayed graphically, rather than through formal equations or some other (generally less understandable) means. Below in figure 4.1, an example of a generic structural model that might be used to analyze citizen satisfaction data, along with a detailed example produced with

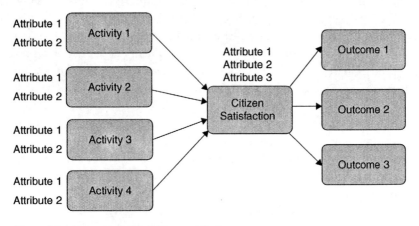

Figure 4.1 A generic model of citizen satisfaction.

actual data, are provided. (In figure A.1 in the appendix, we provide a more technically rigorous presentation of this SEM model.)

Before proceeding, a few comments on the nature and genesis of this "generic" model of citizen satisfaction are necessary, as this model arrangement is supported by substantial prior research and theory.

Performance measurement through satisfaction measurement is an area of intense interest for many organizations, a development we have discussed (at least to some extent) in all of the previous chapters. The private sector took the lead in creating models of consumer-centric performance measurement, but these models have increasingly been adapted and applied to citizen experiences with government as well, and employed to explore the experiences behind the formation of citizen attitudes—and especially citizen satisfaction—with this class of services. Thus, and as is the case for profit-making, private sector companies, the language and proverbs of "citizen satisfaction" pervade many government organizations today.

While conceptual and empirical models of citizen satisfaction with government services continue to vary across organizations and between researchers (i.e., particular model specifications defining precisely what influences the formation of citizen satisfaction attitudes, the ideal way to measure satisfaction, the most important outcomes of citizen satisfaction, etc.), and almost certainly always will, a majority of academic studies on the topic adopt some version of what can be called the "performance-satisfaction-trust" model.[12] This approach adopts a simple yet logical, theoretically grounded, and well-tested perspective on defining the manner in which satisfaction judgments are formed, identifying various citizen perceptions of government performance as the primary determinants of citizen satisfaction, and in turn positioning satisfaction as an intermediate or moderating variable and the primary predictor of the most important outcome metrics, often including some measure of citizen trust. In short, it is this basic theoretical construct that defines this—and most—models of citizen satisfaction, encompassing drivers of satisfaction, citizen satisfaction, and outcomes of satisfaction within a single model.

With this in mind, in the generic model example provided above, satisfaction is hypothesized to be driven by certain core experiences (as yet undefined) with a particular government agency or department, and in turn to influence several (again, as yet undefined) outcomes. Thus the graphic squares ("Activity 1," "Activity 2," etc.) reflect variables (multi-item latent variables estimated in our structural model) including pieces of information (variables from survey questions) elicited through our questionnaire, questions that are deemed to be elements within some larger phenomenon. Each "Attribute" reflects one of the survey questions included within the latent variable to which it is assigned. Mean scores are generated for each of these attributes, as well as for the composite, multi-attribute latent variables that combine these attributes (with the latter mean score being *weighted averages of the attributes derived from the attribute's importance within the model*). These mean scores become our key performance indicators reflecting the level of performance for the measured agency along each dimension.

Moreover, the arrows connecting the latent variables represent the path coefficients or direct effects connecting the latent variables, and as in the case of MLR, these coefficients indicate the strength of the predictor-response relationship of the two connected variables, with larger coefficients indicative of a "more important" influencing factor. A latent variable with an arrow leading away from it has been identified as a determinant or driver of the variable at the end of the arrow. For example, "Activity 1" through "Activity 4" have been defined as drivers of satisfaction that can be constructed differently (i.e., composed of different survey questions) in relation to the particular ways an agency or program regularly interacts with its population of citizens. As discussed in the last chapter, while these activities are likely to vary across agencies and programs depending on their core mission or the ways they interface with citizens (e.g., regulatory agencies often have vastly different missions and goals than benefits-providing agencies, and thus interact differently with citizens), items such as information delivery, process, and customer service are often good candidates for factors influencing citizen satisfaction, because activities performed by a significant majority of government agencies and departments. Likewise, the undefined outcomes on the right side of the model ("Outcome 1" through "Outcome 3") can vary across agencies as well, but often include factors like trust, confidence, compliance, recommendation, complaint behavior, and so forth.

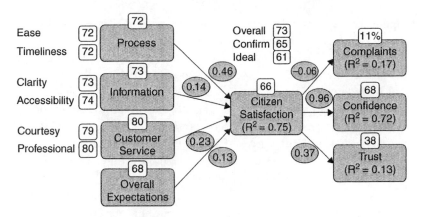

Figure 4.2 An example citizen satisfaction model with output.

Note: All coefficients/path estimates significant at P<0.001.

The completed model in figure 4.2, which now includes all of the defined latent variables (on the left- and right-hand sides), along with the mean scores, coefficients, and some additional output as well, provides an example of a fully completed model ready for interpretation by the researcher.

While we will go into considerably more detail and discuss a variety of useful tools for interpreting these results in a fashion that can help guide strategic decision making in chapter 5, some broad interpretations of this complete SEM model are required, as this exercise will lay the groundwork for the more in-depth interpretative exercises provided in the next chapter.

In this completed model, the mean scores for both the individual survey items/attributes (survey questions)—which were asked on a 1–10 scale during interviewing—and the latent variables have been transformed to a 0–100 scale during analysis for ease of interpretation.[13] The scores for the individual questions within the latent variables (e.g., "courtesy" of Customer Service at 79, "clarity" of information at 73, "ease" of the Process experienced at 72, and so forth) reflect performance based on the average response of the respondents in the survey for each separate survey question. The scores for the latent variables are weighted averages of the mean scores for the individual variables included therein, and reflect performance on these overall activities (Process at 72, Customer Service at 80, Satisfaction at 66, etc.).[14] In all cases, because of how the questions are worded in the survey, a higher score indicates better or stronger performance, with the obvious exception of Complaints, which is the percentage of respondents (11%) that indicated having formally complained to the government agency they experienced, and where (at least superficially) a smaller number is considered preferable.

In this example model, four variables in the model are hypothesized to influence Citizen Satisfaction: Process, Information, Customer Service, and Citizen Expectations. Two of these variables, Process (0.46) and Customer Service (0.23), have significantly larger effects on Citizen Satisfaction according to the coefficients on the arrows, which (as in the case of MLR) indicate the model's predicted effect of a 1-point change in the independent variable on Citizen Satisfaction, and thus a larger number again indicates a stronger relationship. And because of these larger effects—which suggest that as these activities increase in performance, so too will satisfaction increase relatively more—these two predictor variables provide good candidates for focusing improvement efforts with the goal of increasing satisfaction. Citizen Expectations and Information have smaller (but not insignificant) effects, suggesting that while these areas are not entirely irrelevant to satisfaction, improvements in these areas are less likely to have a large positive impact on Citizen Satisfaction.[15]

Furthermore, the three right-hand side variables, outcomes of Citizen Satisfaction and citizen perceptions hypothesized in this model to be influenced by satisfaction, are all single-item survey questions, with scores and coefficients provided as before. The complaint rate of 11 percent shows that roughly that proportion of the respondents included in the sample complained, and the small but negative coefficient (−0.06) indicates that as satisfaction increases, the complaint rate will decline. The two trust variables (one for confidence in the particular agency experienced, the other for trust in the federal government overall) are scored on the 0–100 scale like the other model variables. The Confidence variable (at 68) scores substantially higher than the Trust variable (at only 38), suggesting that citizens have much higher levels of confidence in individual agencies than they have trust in the federal government as a whole. Citizen Satisfaction has a significant effect on all three outcome variables, as expected, but is most influential in determining the citizens' confidence in the agency and trust in government overall, as shown by the comparatively larger coefficients. In other words, the model predicts that as Citizen Satisfaction increases, both Confidence in the agency experienced and Trust in the government overall will also increase significantly, an important finding that speaks to the importance of satisfaction measurement and improvement as a means to this vital end. In the next chapter, we will use the coefficient connecting Citizen Satisfaction and Trust as an important element in a strategy for prioritizing government-wide satisfaction improvement.

Finally, within each independent variable (or at least each "endogenous" variable, or variable that has an arrow leading to it), the R^2 statistics show how much of the variance in the variable is explained by the factors that influence it, again just as in MLR. A higher R^2 value closer to 1.0 indicates more explained variance, and thus a "better" result. The high R^2 value for Citizen Satisfaction (0.75) indicates that the four variables that influence it predict about 75 percent of the movement or variance in Satisfaction, a positive result indicating a solid model that tells us a good deal about why and how satisfaction varies. The right-hand, outcome side variables show lower R^2 values (with the exception of Confidence), but this is

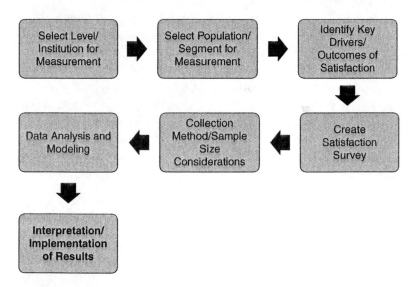

Figure 4.3 A satisfaction measurement flow chart.

largely because all three are hypothesized to be directly influenced by a single predictor variable only, Citizen Satisfaction.

While we will leave explanation of the model and its statistics for now, the next chapter is devoted to a variety of interpretational tools and uses of this data that will further clarify how these statistics can be employed to make strategic decisions about process improvement. More specifically, the next chapter explores how the few important pieces of data explained here—the mean scores and the coefficients linking the variables—can be interpreted to determine the level of an agency's performance (either relative to itself over time, or relative to some other agency), identifying areas in need of improvement that will have the greatest positive impact on citizen satisfaction, how both scores and impacts can be benchmarked across agencies toward discovering best practices, and other related topics.

Conclusion

This chapter has provided an overview of some statistical techniques that can be used to examine satisfaction survey data. We have highlighted and provided the most explanation of the SEM methods, a technique preferred by many involved in the analysis of this kind of data (see figure 4.3 for a flow chart summarizing the steps in chapters three and four). In the next chapter, we expand on many of the themes discussed above, providing a variety of practical examples for how satisfaction and related data can be utilized toward achieving the primary purposes and objectives of this practice—including enhancing accountability and transparency, realizing process and service quality improvements, benchmarking for comparative determination of performance and identifying best practices, and so on.

CHAPTER 5

Using Citizen Satisfaction Results: A Multidimensional Priority Matrix Approach for Satisfaction Improvement

Introduction

In the last chapter, we examined several statistical techniques—including one robust and preferable method, in our estimation, known as structural equation modeling—for analyzing citizen satisfaction data. Using these techniques, we illustrated how satisfaction data, once collected, can be analyzed with the goal of creating action-oriented output, and explained the nature of this statistical output. In this chapter we take the next step and provide some practical examples using real satisfaction data and results and interpreting this data with the goal of devising strategies for improving processes and services in a manner conducive to improved citizen satisfaction. More specifically, using simple tools like the well-known "priority matrix," we begin by examining how satisfaction data combined with these tools can aid researchers in identifying those areas that should be viewed as focal points in trying to improve citizen perceptions of government performance. We then discuss how this data can also be used to benchmark performance across agencies toward identifying governmental performance leaders and the "best practices" responsible for strong performance, again relying on actual data and results to illustrate these techniques.

Finally, we close the chapter by moving from the micro to the macro level, and illustrate one technique for how this data—if available across a sufficient number of the most important government programs, agencies, and departments—can be aggregated-up to help define a government-wide strategy for prioritizing improvements aimed at optimal citizen satisfaction across the entirety of a large, complex, multilevel governmental system tasked with serving millions of citizens in diverse ways. From this perspective and using these methods, satisfaction data can be employed by national-level governments—or by related organizations, such as oversight groups or legislatures, for instance—to most efficiently improve *all* of their programs and services (or at least the most important programs and services) in a way that maximizes citizen satisfaction and trust with the government and across the largest number of citizens possible.

Interpreting Satisfaction Results

The Priority Matrix: A Primer

For many of those reading this book who work in data analysis, statistics, consulting, government research, and similar and related professions, the priority matrix tool will be a recognizable one that needs little description. But because this tool will be used extensively throughout the remainder of this chapter, and in multiple distinct ways that may be somewhat new and unfamiliar even to readers otherwise knowledgeable about the basic purposes of the tool, a brief review of its core elements is necessary.

The general concept of the priority matrix was first outlined in the 1960s as an element of computer and machine programming, a method for instructing these systems to automatically perform certain tasks before others (to "prioritize" them) based on the programmer's predetermination of the relative importance of these tasks.[1] Today, while still certainly used as an element in programming, the priority matrix concept is elicited just as frequently (if not more so, it sometimes seems) outside the computer sciences proper. In general, this tool is employed to help the researcher or analyst, and often the managers and policymakers responsible for rendering final decisions, better understand which tasks are most important and need to be completed immediately, which are important but do not require

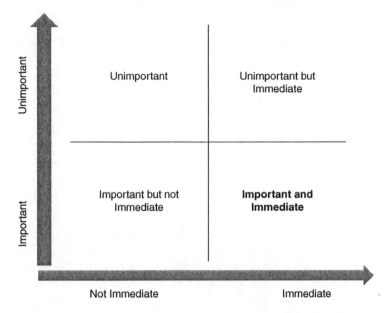

Figure 5.1   A general priority matrix.

immediate attention, and those tasks that are relatively unimportant. By way of illustration, a generic priority matrix is presented in
figure 5.1.

Simply put, and as the above graphic should help clarify, this priority matrix in its simple, two-dimensional form is designed to help
us categorize a set of tasks (really, any set of tasks) based on two categories: the overall importance of the task, and the time-sensitivity
of the task. By way of brief example, let us imagine we have four
tasks (at this point, randomly ordered tasks) on our "to-do" list on
some weekday morning: (1) watch the morning news; (2) vacuum the
trunk of the car; (3) get the kids to school; and (4) shop for grocer-
ies. In order to help us decide how best to accomplish these tasks,
and to determine the order in which we will complete them, we
might turn to a priority matrix and place each task in one of the four
quadrants based on a determination of that task's importance and
time-sensitivity. In doing so, we would most likely assign getting
the kids to school to the "important and immediate" quadrant (the
bottom-right quadrant), as the task is both of high importance and

time-sensitive (assuming, of course, that the prioritizer values both education and having their kids arrive to school on time, as many/most people do).

Likewise, we might place grocery shopping in the "important but not immediate" quadrant (bottom-left quadrant), because while food is vital for the family's survival, we are not yet entirely out of food, we don't have to cook again until dinner, and therefore shopping can be delayed until later in the day. Finally, we would most likely assign watching the morning news to the "not important but immediate" quadrant (top-right quadrant), as it is not a vitally important task but one we would have to do immediately or not at all, and vacuuming the car to the "unimportant" category (top-left quadrant), as it is neither truly vital nor time-sensitive (unless the prioritizer in this instance is unusually sensitive about the cleanliness of his or her trunk). Thus in this simple priority matrix example, our results would tell us to: (1) first get the kids to school, then (2) watch the morning news (but only if the first task is completed early or on-time), then (3) go grocery shopping, and lastly, (4) vacuum the trunk of the car, but again only if time is available after completing the other three tasks.[2]

With this brief explanation of the priority matrix and its purposes at our disposal, we can turn now to its uses vis-à-vis citizen satisfaction data and satisfaction results interpretation. In the context of this type of research, and performance measurement practice in general, the priority matrix tool is most often applied slightly differently, and is typically employed to identify those areas most in need of performance improvement based on the overarching goal of enhancing citizen satisfaction. In this sense, we maintain "importance" as one of the two analytical categories (important, unimportant), but replace time-sensitivity with measures of "performance" (strong/good versus weak/poor performance), which we will define here as performance on satisfaction, some particular attribute or set of attributes that influence satisfaction, or outcomes of satisfaction.

Now, referring back to the model of citizen satisfaction we outlined and discussed in some detail in chapter 4, and when analyzed using the techniques we described there, satisfaction data produces an array of useful statistical outputs, but can and should provide

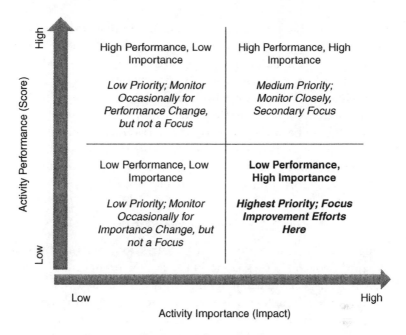

Figure 5.2 A priority matrix for citizen satisfaction data.

two pieces of information we described in that chapter as being most important for data interpretation with practical reforms and process improvements as our objective: scores rating *performance* on some activity that drives satisfaction, and impacts measuring the relative *importance* of an activity or program/service attribute in influencing satisfaction. And it is precisely these two pieces of data that can be analyzed within a priority matrix. Figure 5.2 illustrates how such a citizen satisfaction-data-focused priority matrix is usually arranged.

As this now-updated figure shows, in the context of interpreting satisfaction data toward defining the best, most practical improvements a government agency might make toward efficiently and effectively improving citizen satisfaction, we are really focusing (and will continue to focus below) on activities that fall into one of two quadrants: activities that are important and have strong performance, and activities that are important but perform poorly. The other two quadrants—where performance is either good or bad, but importance is comparatively low—are less relevant, as they mostly warrant only future monitoring for changes that might have made them more relevant, as over time the importance of activities can certainly change.[3] When we return to the priority matrix tool and apply it to analyze and interpret data below, the rationale for this approach should become clearer and these two quadrants will again be deemed most essential, as they will give us insight into the areas and activities where government should turn its attention in improving the citizen satisfaction it delivers to citizens.

A Case Study: Identifying Priorities and Best Practices

Having briefly outlined the priority matrix tool, we turn now to an examination of some satisfaction data and results for a variety of US federal government programs and agencies and, employing this tool, walk through exercises for how to interpret this data and results, with practical reforms aimed at improved satisfaction as our objective. Like most of what has come before and will come later, the data we analyze in these exercises come from the ACSI study, a research project we have previously described in some detail in the "Introduction." The data we analyze in this case study consists of the multiyear survey sample reflecting citizen perceptions measured using a common questionnaire, data previously described and analyzed in chapter 4. In this exercise, however, we focus specifically on only eight large, diverse, high-profile US government programs and agencies—Veterans Affairs (VA), Medicare, the Social Security Administration (SSA), Medicaid, the National Parks Service (NPS), the State Department's Passport Services (PS), the Internal Revenue Service (IRS), and the Department of Agriculture's Food Stamps (FS) program. For the purposes of this exercise, we will approach the data as though our first-order objective were to make changes (reforms) that would best position us to realize *improvements in both the activities that drive satisfaction and citizen satisfaction with the VA and its processes and services.*[4] Yet when we are done with this exercise, the reader will hopefully be able to utilize this same data to render his or her own conclusions about reform targets for the other agencies for which data is provided.

It should be noted that while we use a pooled, multiyear sample of survey responses in this exercise (data collected across multiple sampling periods, or years, and then aggregated and analyzed simultaneously), we do so only to boost the sample sizes for the segments examined—in this case, the agencies and programs mentioned above by name—and thus the statistical reliability and stability of our results.[5] However, most often this kind of analysis would be done using data from a single point-in-time—a single year, a single measurement period such as a fiscal quarter, and so on—as often data of this nature is time-sensitive, and may in fact exhibit a type of "seasonality."[6] Yet because our primary purpose here is to evidence and illustrate in general how a practically focused use of the data might be accomplished, this pooled sample should prove more than sufficient.

The statistical results that follow for each government program were generated using the same methods outlined toward the end of the last chapter—producing all of the various output from the structural equation model discussed there—although in this context we present only some of the output, the results most useful for the interpretive exercises that follow, and eschew a more detailed review of the methods. But should the reader require a refresher in how these scores and effects were produced, the last chapter should be referenced (along with the appendix). And so to begin, two tables (tables 5.1 and 5.2) complete with data are presented and described

Table 5.1 Variable scores/performance (0–100 scale)

	VA	Medicare	SSA	Medicaid	NPS	Passport	IRS	FS
Satisfaction	69	72	70	65	80	71	57	61
Expectations	71	70	69	66	79	69	59	62
Information	74	75	76	69	87	77	66	72
Ease of Info	*74*	*78*	*76*	*69*	*87*	*77*	*68*	*72*
Clarity of Info	*74*	*73*	*76*	*69*	*88*	*78*	*64*	*73*
Process	68	78	74	65	87	72	67	66
Timeliness of Process	*68*	*77*	*75*	*66*	*87*	*71*	*68*	*67*
Ease of Process	*69*	*80*	*73*	*64*	*87*	*72*	*67*	*65*
Customer Service	85	81	80	76	93	79	78	71
Courtesy of Personnel	*85*	*81*	*80*	*75*	*93*	*80*	*78*	*70*
Professionalism of Personnel	*85*	*80*	*80*	*77*	*92*	*79*	*78*	*72*

below. These tables focus on two different statistics, those statistics we discussed in the last chapter and described as "most important," and that will provide the foundation for our priority matrix analysis, with these numbers segmented by the eight programs/agencies mentioned earlier.

Table 5.1 presents the *variable scores or measures of performance* for our eight government agencies on a common set of variables reflecting activities many or most citizens experience when interacting with one of these US federal government agencies. We have, for the purposes of this exercise, defined these activities as the most vital and relevant—but (importantly) still generic and comparable across this otherwise quite diverse set of programs and citizen experiences[7]—predictors of citizen satisfaction. In other words, it is these variables that we have anticipated (during questionnaire design and model conceptualization) will have an important, meaningful effect on satisfaction. These variables were all described in the last chapter, but as a reminder, they reflect (from top to bottom) questions tapping-into the respondents' satisfaction with a federal government agency (measured now as a three-item latent variable including items on overall satisfaction, confirmation/disconfirmation of expectations, and comparison to an ideal), the citizen's prior expectations about their experiences, the ease of accessing information and the clarity of the information accessed (modeled in the Information latent variable), the timeliness and ease of completing the process experienced (modeled in the Process latent variable), and the courtesy and professionalism of the personnel interacted with (modeled in the Customer Service latent variable). As described in the last chapter, all of these variables have been transformed from the 1–10 scale used during interviewing to 0–100 index scores for easier interpretation, and the data in the chart reflects a weighted mean (average) score for each latent variable and each agency, with the weights derived from the statistical techniques we use to analyze the data, and an unweighted mean score for the individual variables included in each latent.

Because VA will serve as our focus in these exercises, this agency's scores are bolded and appear in the far left column for easier referencing. And as the table shows, VA registers a mean satisfaction score of 69, with the other variables (including both the manifest (raw or survey) variables and the latent variables), those items identified here as the drivers or primary factors influencing citizen satisfaction, ranging in score from a low of 68 (for both timeliness of the process, and the Process latent overall) to a high of 85 (for both of the customer service variables, and the Customer Service latent variable overall). In addition to these scores for VA, scores for the same variables for all of the additional agencies mentioned earlier are also included, and show a wide interagency range in performance on these attributes and activities from the high 50s (for the IRS) to the low 90s (for the NPS). Once again, and as we will make clear below, the purpose of this first type of statistic is to not only examine mean scores of performance on satisfaction and the other variables for any one particular agency, but also to compare performance on those items that influence satisfaction across agencies, and eventually to use this as part of a calculus for identifying practice and performance leaders.

Table 5.2 presents the regression coefficients—or what we have alternatively called drivers, impacts or effects elsewhere—for the same eight programs. Rather than showing the level of performance on these variables for each agency, this data shows the *strength of the relationship between each of these influencing factors and satisfaction*. Like the scores presented above, these coefficients were produced using the structural equation model and methods outlined in the last chapter. For the sake of simplicity, rather than examine the data

Table 5.2   Impacts/importance (effect of a 1-point change on satisfaction)

	VA	Medicare	SSA	Medicaid	NPS	Passport	IRS	FS
Expectations	0.05	0.23	0.09	0.17	0.08	0.07	0.16	0.21
Information	0.20	0.00	0.30	0.00	0.45	0.15	0.20	0.00
Ease of Info	0.10	0.00	0.14	0.00	0.23	0.08	0.10	0.00
Clarity of Info	0.10	0.00	0.15	0.00	0.22	0.07	0.10	0.00
Process	0.48	0.55	0.39	0.45	0.25	0.36	0.40	0.50
Timeliness of Process	0.24	0.27	0.19	0.23	0.12	0.17	0.20	0.28
Ease of Process	0.23	0.28	0.20	0.21	0.13	0.20	0.20	0.22
Customer Service	0.25	0.15	0.21	0.30	0.15	0.44	0.21	0.12
Courtesy of Personnel	0.12	0.07	0.11	0.15	0.07	0.19	0.11	0.06
Professionalism of Personnel	0.12	0.08	0.11	0.16	0.08	0.24	0.11	0.06

as it is often displayed in the form of full graphic models, complete with latent variables and scores, model effects, and assorted other output, as we did in the last chapter, here we provide only the effects or coefficients for these latent variables (as well as the manifest variables contained therein) as they relate to the latent citizen satisfaction variable.

Each of the coefficients shown above, starting again on the left-hand side with our focal program In this exercise, VA, reflect the predicted effect between each variable and citizen satisfaction, or the predicted effect of a 1-point change in each of these variables (both manifest and latent) on satisfaction, holding all of the other predictors constant; the larger the number, the larger the effect the variable has on satisfaction. For VA, for example, these results show that the model predicts that a 1-point change (improvement) in the Process latent variable (from 68 to 69 on the 0–100 scale) would result in an increase in satisfaction of 0.48 points, from 69 to 69.48. An even bigger change of, for instance, 5 points in Process (which is obviously a larger but not unreasonable target improvement in this kind of exercise) would improve satisfaction from 69 to 71.4, a very substantial and meaningful increase in satisfaction. And again, while the scores shown earlier will provide our metric of performance (how is an agency doing on Activity X, Y, and Z?), these impacts will function as the measures of the *relative importance* of the activities that drive satisfaction (which activity is more or most important in driving citizen satisfaction?).

With this outline of these two types of statistics at our disposal, we turn now to how this data can be utilized to "populate" a priority matrix, with the goal of helping the analyst determine which activities or areas a government program might focus on in its efforts to improve the citizen-user experience. In the priority matrix in figure 5.3 below, the scores on the latent variables identified as influencing satisfaction have been treated as our measures of performance, while the coefficients or impacts have been used to rate the importance of these variables, with this data used to complete the matrix.

As this now-complete priority matrix for VA illustrates, there are some areas where the program is performing well, and some where

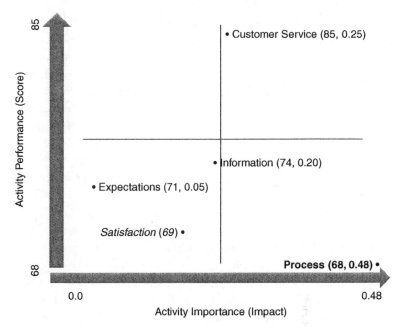

Figure 5.3 The priority matrix for Veterans Affairs.

substantial room for improvement exists. Likewise, some of the measured variables are substantially more important, in terms of the size of the effect these activities have on satisfaction, than others.[8] Indeed, these results show a fairly "normal" priority matrix, with activities spread-out across the quadrants in the matrix, and some fairly clear conclusions in terms of priorities.

Beginning on the lower left-hand side of the matrix, we see one activity (not including the score for Satisfaction, which appears in the matrix only for comparative and reference purposes) that we would clearly categorize as "lower priority": citizen expectations prior to the experience with VA. In this instance, we would identify improvements here as a lower priority because, while the variable scores relatively poorly in terms of performance, and could therefore stand improvement in the eyes of citizens (in other words, citizens expect relatively little from VA prior to the experience), expectations also have a relatively small impact on satisfaction. Because of this, improvements to expectations, if they were to be sought and achieved, are unlikely to have a significant effect—or at least as large an effect—as would improvements in any of the other identified and measured activities and attributes. Therefore, expectations would be categorized, referring back to our "Priority Matrix for Citizen Satisfaction Data," as a low priority area to monitor for change (either in performance or importance), but not as an area to focus on immediately in an effort to improve satisfaction with VA.

Less clear in terms of interpretation is the Information latent variable, which appears to "straddle" the lower left-hand and lower right-hand quadrants in the matrix. While the variable performs better than most of the others in terms of score (74), this score is still fairly low when compared, for instance, to the Customer Service latent variable (which we discuss next). It also scores fairly poorly when compared to the Information score for most of the other agencies for which data is provided in table 5.1, meaning that VA does a relatively poor job providing information even when compared with other agencies. Furthermore, while the variable has a larger effect on Satisfaction than Expectations, its effect is slightly smaller than Customer Service, and substantially smaller than Process. Additional interpretation of this variable—and its priority as a potential reform target for improving VA's citizen satisfaction—is provided below.

Turning now to the right-hand side of the matrix, and here we arrive at the area of greatest interest, the activities that we—or in our example, researchers and managers within the VA working to improve the citizen-user experience and the agency's satisfaction— might be best served in focusing. In the top right-hand quadrant of the matrix, one activity is represented: the customer service provided by VA to its citizen-users. This activity has a fairly strong impact on Satisfaction (second only to Process, and slightly larger than Information), suggesting that it is a comparatively more important factor in influencing it. However, Customer Service also scores relatively well, meaning that, while important, and definitely something that should at least be closely monitored going forward (as a decline in the score for this variable could have a negative impact on Satisfaction), improvements here may be harder to realize. That is, because the variable already scores well relative to other indicators for VA (and indeed, as table 5.1 shows, relative to almost all of the other programs and agencies we are investigating here), there is simply less room for improvement, reducing the attractiveness of this as a focal-point activity for reform; as the variable already scores well, improvements may be more difficult to achieve, based on the premise that it is typically more difficult to make even marginal improvements in areas currently performing at a high level.

Finally, in the bottom right-hand quadrant of the matrix we find one activity that both scores poorly (lowest among the measured activities) and has a strong (the strongest) effect on Satisfaction: the Process variable, measuring the ease and timeliness of VA's processes. Referring back to our generic "Priority Matrix for Citizen Satisfaction Data," the logic of focusing first and foremost on this activity as a means for improving satisfaction should now be clear: as the variable scores poorly and registers the strongest impact on satisfaction, this activity provides the most fertile ground for seeking stronger citizen satisfaction through reform efforts. That is, the lower score for the variable suggests more room for improvement, and perhaps easier improvements, than, for instance, the aforementioned Customer Service variable, which has a reasonably large impact on satisfaction but already scores well. Furthermore, the stronger impact suggests that any improvements realized in the activity will likely yield a larger positive effect on satisfaction than similar improvements to any of the other measured activities, which (regardless of how they score) all have smaller impacts on satisfaction.

Therefore, based on the statistics presented above and the categorization of the data in our priority matrix, we would conclude that focusing on the Process (as the timeliness and the ease of the VA's application processes) would most likely result in the biggest "bang for the buck" in terms of improving satisfaction. Based on our analysis, this is the lowest-performing/highest-impact area likely to give us the best return-on-investment vis-à-vis enhanced citizen satisfaction. Furthermore, the priority matrix reveals that a secondary focus behind Process is the Information variable and its activities, rather than Customer Service (which might normally be viewed as a secondary focus). That is, while Information scores better and has a lower impact than Process, it is nonetheless an attractive secondary focus because the lower score (relative to some of the other measured activities for VA, and when compared to the Information scores for

Table 5.3 Priority matrix conclusions for Veterans Affairs

Activity	Action
Process	*Highest Priority: Lowest score/largest impact data combination recommends Process as the most important area for focusing improvements aimed at enhanced Citizen Satisfaction with VA.*
Information	*Medium Priority: Low score and fairly strong impact makes this an area where potential improvements might be sought, but second to Process.*
Customer Service	*Lower Priority: Monitor and seek to maintain current level of performance only, as the very high score likely makes improvements more difficult.*
Expectations	*Lowest Priority: Monitor for performance or importance changes, but not a focal activity.*

some of the other measured programs and agencies) provides room for improvement, and the moderate impact suggests that improvements here could have a real effect on Satisfaction. And as mentioned earlier, Information is a more attractive focal point in this case than Customer Service, which is less appealing because of its already very high score (better than all the other agencies in table 5.1 with the exception of NPS). Table 5.3 encapsulates our conclusions in regards to citizen satisfaction improvements for VA from our priority matrix.

But is there anything in the additional data displayed earlier (in tables 5.1 and 5.2) that might help us in terms of learning *how* VA might go about improving these particular activities? Let us turn now to the practice of performance benchmarking as one method for this kind of inter-organizational learning. As we described in chapter 2, performance benchmarking can be defined as, like we originally quoted there, the practice of identifying "competitive targets which render the weak points of the benchmarking organization visible and *to establish means of improvement*" [my italics]. In other words, the central purpose of benchmarking, beyond using this as a tool for comparing across organizations or government programs towards better understanding relative performance on satisfaction or some other activity, an important task in its own right, is to seek information from the "benchmarking partners" that might reveal *strategies for improvement,* to identify how some agencies are able to do a comparatively better job delivering some service or performing on some other activities.[9]

Staying with our present example, our goal is to seek one (or a few) benchmarking partners for VA that can help us understand how the agency might improve the ease and timeliness of its application processes as a way of improving citizens' perceptions of performance on the Process variable overall, and thereby improving citizen satisfaction. In this sense, we would want to identify a government agency that, like VA, exhibits a strong effect between Process and Satisfaction, but one that also shows stronger performance or a better score in Process than VA. Referring back to the two tables of results provided and discussed earlier and we can use this data to create a new priority matrix, one that focuses across all eight programs and populates the matrix with the Process scores and impacts for each. This new priority matrix is provided below in figure 5.4.

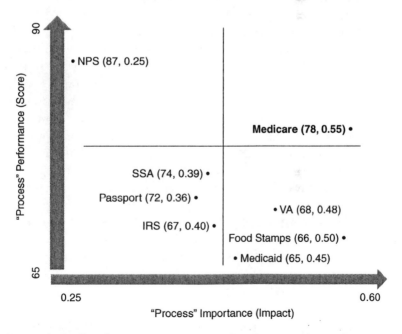

Figure 5.4 Benchmarking priority matrix: "Process" performance and impact by agency.

Examining this matrix and seeking another federal government program where Process has a similarly strong impact on Satisfaction, but which scores significantly better on this activity, and we find one such program in the top right-hand quadrant—Medicare. All of the data for Medicare is, not coincidentally, displayed directly next to the data for VA in tables 5.1 and 5.2. With an impact of 0.55, Process for Medicare has a similar but even slightly stronger effect on Satisfaction when compared to VA. However, the respondents who have experienced these processes for Medicare rate these activities much higher (both the timeliness and the ease of the processes), leading to an overall Process score of 78, 10 points higher than the same score for VA. In sum, the results show that citizens who have interacted with these two programs—both of which are, importantly, mostly responsible for administering an application process for benefits delivery to certain groups of citizens—indicate that, for both, the ease and timeliness of the application process are the most important drivers of satisfaction, but that Medicare receives substantially higher ratings in these areas.

And so, based on the findings from this performance benchmarking process, we would begin to ask questions about how Medicare "does things better" than VA, or at least how and why Medicare's respondents seem to indicate that this is the case, and how this might inform researchers and managers within VA in improving their own Process performance as a means for improving Satisfaction. This question-asking might take the form of a purely qualitative process, but could also involve a distinct data collection and analysis effort. But regardless, the questions asked here might include things like: Is Medicare's advantage simply a matter of faster application processing? If so, is this faster processing driven by a smaller workload, or is it due to a larger or better trained staff? Are the forms easier to understand and simpler to complete? If so, is there a way VA can simplify its application? Perhaps Medicare has done a better job mastering information technology in a way that makes these processes more user-friendly? Or, could it be that Medicare's advantage is due to something that may not help VA improve its processes, like the total number of new applicants each year, the percentage of applicants who have their application approved (due to policies enacted by the political system rather than the agency itself), or the relative age of the respondents rating the application process (as older respondents have been shown to give higher satisfaction ratings on average, if only slightly)?[10] While we will leave these question unanswered for now, the series of steps we have outlined can provide a good blueprint for how satisfaction data can and should be analyzed, prioritized, and benchmarked with real, practical improvements in processes and services as the goal.

To be clear, even after all of the exercises we have walked through above, we may very well not yet be at the end of the research road for VA in seeking stronger citizen satisfaction. While the suggestion that "VA must improve the ease and timeliness of the application process" gives a solid starting point for focusing on just a few particular, "most important" activities requiring improvements that will be conducive to higher satisfaction, and while benchmarking has helped us identify at least some possible sources of information for organizational learning in seeking strategies for actually improving these attributes (which we found in Medicare), completing this task for VA in a manner that is both effective and resource efficient is almost certainly more complex. Indeed, these findings may represent just the start to a second stage of the research project, one where VA "drills-down" into a range of more particular dimensions related to the application process—the length, complexity and language of the paperwork that needs to be completed, the website that is available for completing the application, and so forth—and then does further data collection and modeling (similar to the kind of questionnaire design, data collection, and statistical modeling we have already done, but with a greater degree of specificity to VA itself) to identify where improvements in these more specific areas would best be served. Yet regardless, these activities have set us down a much clearer path, and have helped us look in the right places and ask the right questions about how VA might improve.

One final caveat about interpreting citizen satisfaction data, one specifically concerning the practice of cross-agency benchmarking for comparing scores, seeking practice leaders, and so forth, is necessary. In the exercises pursued above, we have treated the data for all of the programs and agencies discussed somewhat indifferently in terms of each agency's core mission. That is, we have compared the performance of a wide range of agencies and programs that seek very different objectives, from the IRS, which pursues a decidedly unpopular regulatory mission (tax collection), to benefits providers like VA and SSA, to service providers like NPS (which mostly provides low-cost access to highly popular tourist destinations). Yet these kinds of comparisons always need to be done carefully, with a conscious understanding that they can only be taken so far. For instance, it would be unwise to compare satisfaction scores across all of these programs and agencies and render a judgment about "who is doing better" on this basis alone, without acknowledging that satisfaction performance for these agencies is undoubtedly influenced by what they are tasked by the political system with accomplishing. The nature of the mission pursued by different programs, agencies and departments must be considered when comparing performance on any of the variables represented above, as it is unrealistic to expect a tax collection agency which takes citizens' money with agencies asked only to give benefits or offer popular and nearly free services. In the next chapter, we return to the issue of the relationship between citizens' perceptions of government performance and agency mission.

Similarly, the measures of importance we have examined above must also be considered in the context of the purpose or mission of the government agency, as the particular ways that government agencies choose (or are required) to interface with citizens may be guided by its mission, and in turn, some comparisons may have little real validity or usefulness. For instance, while it may be interesting to know that the NPS scores a very high 87 for Process, a far stronger score than that received by any of the other agencies for which data is available, it is unlikely that there exists enough in common between the rigors and complexity of the tax-filing process at IRS and the process of reserving a campground site (for example) for too much inter-organizational learning to occur here; telling IRS to improve its processes by "doing what the NPS does" is an extreme oversimplification that would help the IRS only a little or not at all. In short, the selection of benchmarking partners must always be completed with care, and nothing we have suggested above should lead the researcher to conclude otherwise.

Government-Wide Performance Improvement Prioritization

As we have discussed in this chapter, in portions of several earlier chapters, and as we will discuss to some extent in the chapters that follow, an undeniably essential goal of citizen satisfaction measurement is to aid individual government agencies and programs in improving the services they deliver to citizens. With any luck, through the efforts of the last several chapters, the reader is now convinced about both the importance and the feasibility of these ventures; government programs can use this data to improve the satisfaction of their own citizen-users in an effective and efficient way. Moreover, as we outlined in chapter 1, it would seem that governments at all levels in the United States and across the globe almost universally agree with the central importance of these activities for creating better, more pleasing experiences for citizens, as the abundance of recent initiatives focused on this sort of activity would seem to attest.

Yet at least one important question still remains: Can citizen satisfaction data help guide a broader, government-wide agenda for performance improvement? That is, from at least one perspective, an agency- or program-centric view of performance and citizen satisfaction improvement could be viewed as too narrow or insufficient. After all, while central governments certainly must care about the performance of each of the discrete, individual administrative agencies they oversee, they must also care—and in some cases, perhaps care even more—about the performance of the *government as a whole*, along with citizen perceptions of and satisfaction with this larger, more abstract entity.[11] (For instance, as we discussed in chapter 2 and discuss in more detail in chapter 6, national governments worldwide have seen aggregate citizen trust in government decline, and as such have had to become aware of and concerned with this type of broader, diffuse citizen attitude.) And as we discussed in our case study earlier, just as efficiently improving satisfaction within a particular agency necessitates focusing on some activities over others, so to may it be the case that a government-wide approach to performance improvement will require focusing on some agencies or programs over others. So again, the question that remains is: How (if at all) can central, national-level governments use satisfaction data and some of the tools presented thus far to not only improve overall satisfaction with the government, but to do so in an efficient way that emphasizes improvements in the "most important" programs and agencies over others, those where the resultant impact will be greatest?

To provide one answer to this question, let us leave our objective of determining focal activities for performance improvement at the program level and turn to a macro, government-wide approach where our primary objective is *improving satisfaction and trust in the government overall*. To do so, we begin by providing some additional data in table 5.4:

In table 5.4, three pieces of data are provided for each of the eight programs and agencies we have discussed thus far. First, we reproduce the Citizen Satisfaction score for each agency, starting on the left-hand side with the IRS. In addition, we provide data regarding the total number of annual citizen-users for each of these programs/agencies, with a description of how this total customer population figure was calculated in the notes below the table. Finally, an additional regression coefficient or effect from our SEM statistical model results is provided, in this case, the coefficient that links Citizen Satisfaction to the variable measuring overall trust in the US federal government in Washington, DC (Trust). And with this data, we will again create a priority matrix like those constructed earlier,

Table 5.4 Satisfaction, total citizen-customers, and satisfaction's importance in driving trust

	IRS[a]	NPS[b]	SSA[c]	Medicare[d]	Medicaid[e]	FS[f]	Passport[g]	VA[h]
Satisfaction	57	80	70	72	65	61	71	69
Population (million)	177.3	278.9	57.1	49.4	62	47	13.1	21.5
Trust in Washington, DC	0.39	0.17	0.43	0.42	0.32	0.11	0.38	0.23

[a] Includes the combined total of all tax returns (individual, corporate, estate, etc.) filed in 2012. Source: www.irs.gov.
[b] Includes total visitors to national parks in 2011, which is inflated by those citizens who visit multiple parks or one park on multiple occasions. Source: www.nps.gov.
[c] Includes all Social Security benefits recipients in 2013. Source: www.ssa.gov.
[d] Includes all Medicare enrollees in 2012. Source: The Kaiser Family Foundation (www.kff.org).
[e] Includes all Medicaid enrollees in 2009. Source: The Kaiser Family Foundation (www.kff.org).
[f] Includes total Food Stamp recipients as of 2013. Source: www.washingtonpost.com.
[g] Includes all passports and passport cards issued in 2012. Source: www.travel.state.gov.
[h] Includes all US veterans as of 2011. Source: www.va.gov.

with Citizen Satisfaction as our measure of performance, but now with both the size of the effect of Satisfaction on Trust and the total number of citizen-users as our (combined) measure of importance. Figure 5.5 below illustrates this new priority matrix.[12]

In this instance, and much like the VA-focused exercises provided above, in figure 5.5 we are seeking relatively poor-performers that may serve as good candidates for focusing improvement efforts. But in this case, rather than seeking just poor-performing *activities*, we seek poor-performing programs or agencies in terms of Citizen Satisfaction, driven by the same basic logic that something that performs poorly often provides the best place to turn in seeking improvements that can be more easily realized. Moreover, and again as with the exercises above, we are seeking programs or agencies that not only perform relatively poorly but are also comparatively more important, and will thereby help us accomplish our goal of government-wide satisfaction and trust improvement most effectively and efficiently. As such, here we define importance as those agencies

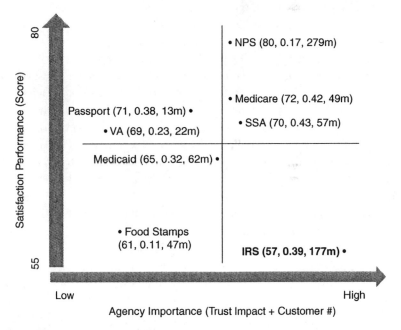

Figure 5.5   A government-wide benchmarking priority matrix: Satisfaction, trust, and total citizen-customers.

where improvements in Citizen Satisfaction are predicted to yield a *larger improvement in Trust,* and will do so for a *comparatively larger number of citizens.*

The logic guiding this particular definition of importance for this exercise is straightforward. On the one hand, defining a strong Citizen Satisfaction-Trust linkage as a measure of importance recognizes that any improvements in Satisfaction with such a program or agency will likely yield a relatively larger improvement in Trust, one of our primary objectives. On the other hand, focusing on those agencies that serve a larger number of citizens means that any improvements in Satisfaction and/or Trust will have a greater impact on aggregate actual satisfaction and trust across society, simply by virtue of the fact that more people will "feel" these improvements. In sum, we are looking within our priority matrix for agencies that have a low-performance/high-importance combination, and therefore, the one or few agencies that have comparatively lower satisfaction, serve a larger number of citizens, and where improvements in satisfaction are predicted to yield a larger impact on trust.

A review of the results provided in table 5.4 and figure 5.5 suggest that, all other things being equal, some programs and agencies are indeed better candidates for focusing improvement efforts than others, assuming our goal is to improve overall satisfaction and trust in the federal government society-wide, and to do so as efficiently as possible. First and foremost, the IRS has the lowest satisfaction score, the second largest total user population, and the third largest observed effect between Citizen Satisfaction and Trust, suggesting that performance improvement efforts should focus on, or at minimum absolutely include, the IRS as a priority. That is, any improvements in satisfaction with the IRS will touch a huge number of citizens, thereby increasing aggregate satisfaction with the entire government substantially, and have a similarly large impact on Trust, both because of the larger coefficient connecting Satisfaction and Trust and because of the larger number of citizens impacted.[13]

On the other hand, while Medicare and SSA both have slightly stronger linkages between Satisfaction and Trust than IRS, both score much higher on Satisfaction and serve/interact with far fewer citizen-customers, making them somewhat less attractive focal agencies. Similarly, NPS serves a huge number of American citizens, but shows a fairly small link between Satisfaction and Trust, and already scores very well on Citizen Satisfaction. All three of these agencies would fall into the secondary-focus/monitor-for-changes category, but would not function as the best agencies to focus on immediately towards improving overall satisfaction and trust with the US federal government. Finally, the remaining agencies score both well and poorly on Citizen Satisfaction, but because their importance is low (either in terms of a small Citizen Satisfaction-Trust linkage, a smaller number of citizens served, or both) they all would fall into the less important category for monitoring.

Therefore, while somewhat brief, this discussion shows how the practice of citizen satisfaction measurement might be used to guide a government-wide, centralized satisfaction improvement agenda. Using just citizen satisfaction and trust data, and a small amount of easily accessible external data, we can begin to draw some conclusions about where—that is, on which programs or agencies—the US federal government might focus in improving citizen perceptions with the government as a whole. Assuming the existence of Citizen Satisfaction scores with a large enough group of programs, agencies and departments, a central government oversight agency responsible for performance improvement could fairly easily outline a citizen satisfaction improvement agenda in this way, one that focuses first on those agencies that serve the largest group of citizens and have the greatest leverage over citizen trust in government as a whole.

Before we leave this discussion, a note regarding political ideology is necessary, as it may very well impact the exercise undertaken immediately above. Throughout this book, starting in the "Introduction" chapter and restated elsewhere, we have tried diligently to emphasize the nonpolitical nature of satisfaction measurement. Creating good, efficient, satisfying government should be a concern that transcends affiliation with a particular political party or ideology. And politicians, at least in the US at the federal level, generally seem to agree; over the past few decades, performance measurement initiatives have been championed by left- and right-leaning governments alike.

Nevertheless, in the approach we have outlined for creating a total government satisfaction improvement strategy above—which assigns importance to some agencies over others based on the total number of citizens contacted and the effect of satisfaction with these agencies on overall trust in government—reasonable *political* disagreements could emerge. That is, at its very core, the suggestion that "those agencies that serve more citizens are more important" could be viewed as excessively egalitarian, and an incorrect way to determine program or agency importance. Shouldn't agencies that have a more important mission or objective (however someone might want to define that) be given greater priority? Indeed, shouldn't some groups of citizens be viewed as "more important customers" of the government regardless of their total numbers, perhaps because they pay more taxes, or have greater need for government assistance, or some similar consideration? Many would argue, for instance, that the conclusions above dramatically downplay the vital importance of focusing improvements on the services provided by VA; while VA may not serve as many Americans directly or exhibit as strong a linkage between Satisfaction and Trust, those it does serve have provided the nation an invaluable service (and in many cases, paid a high price in doing so), and therefore focusing first on improving this agency's services even to a smaller number of Americans is justifiable.

While we will again refrain from attempting to enter or moderate these political debates, it is likely that opinions on these issues will vary, and thus so too might particular strategies for weighting importance in a holistic, government-wide approach to citizen satisfaction improvement. In sum, if nothing else, the researcher must be aware that the potential for political disagreements in precisely how the "importance" of a government program or agency is defined are likely to emerge.

Conclusion

In this chapter, we have provided a general blueprint for using citizen satisfaction data in a practical fashion, in a way that allows researchers to advance from an abstract understanding of the causes and consequences of satisfaction, to an actual agenda guiding strategies for improving that performance within government. Using the simple priority matrix tool, we have offered examples of how analyzed satisfaction data can help determine the best areas for focusing improvement efforts. Moreover, we have showed how this data can be "aggregated-up" and, in combination with some additional data, used to outline a government-wide performance improvement strategy aimed at maximizing satisfaction and trust across the government and society as a whole. In the next chapter, we review a wealth of citizen satisfaction findings over a considerable time period, and compare some of these results to private sector results.

CHAPTER 6

Enduring Lessons in Citizen Satisfaction: Trends, Findings, and Public-Private Comparisons

Introduction

To this point in the book, we have focused primarily on the theory, concepts, and methods central to citizen satisfaction measurement. Moreover, in the last chapter we built on these topics and reviewed some reasonably simple, straightforward techniques for interpreting satisfaction data with organizational and process improvements as our primary goal, examining how this data can be employed toward identifying government agency improvements aimed at enhancing actual performance and citizens' satisfaction with that performance. In this chapter we shift directions toward an investigation of some general but nonetheless vital findings gleaned from citizen satisfaction data. Examining a large sample of data collected and analyzed over multiple years, the primary goal of this chapter is to consider some enduring lessons about citizens' satisfaction with government performance, and to examine these findings both over time and in relation to comparable private sector results.

In what follows, we present a series of what we will call "lessons." Numbering seven in all, these lessons reflect some of the most consistent, interesting (at least in our opinion) and important findings from nearly two decades of research and analysis into citizen satisfaction. Indeed, given the breadth and depth of the data analyzed here, and the consistency of these findings across contexts and over earlier time periods, these lessons reflect something closer to "enduring truths" than mere "results and findings." Furthermore, while we focus primarily on satisfaction with US federal government services, and to a lesser extent on local government services, many of these findings do (or at minimum, could and should) apply equally well to both other levels and types of government in the United States, and in many cases, to governments in other nations as well. But unlike our primary goal in the last two chapters, which aimed at using satisfaction data to draw "smaller," more incremental, and organization-focused lessons about government performance improvement, here we examine "bigger" lessons about government as a whole that can be gleaned from this type of data.

Lessons in Citizen Satisfaction

- *Lesson #1: On average, the private sector provides significantly more satisfaction to consumers than the public sector provides to citizens.*

For most readers, the claim that government is not as satisfying as the free market private sector will come as little surprise. Indeed, evidence that a substantial quantity of data suggests—and has consistently suggested, with very few exceptions—that citizens are less happy with their experiences with the government than they are with their experiences with private sector goods and services will likely serve only to reinforce negative perceptions held by many about government, what it does, and how well it performs. Yet this lesson deserves deeper analysis nonetheless, both because data seem to confirm the opinions and intuitions held by many, but also because the story may be more complex than critics of government would have us believe. First, consider figure 6.1, which presents five years of federal government, local government, and private sector satisfaction data:

Using the same 0–100, low-to-high scale we have referred to in previous chapters (and will use throughout this chapter, unless otherwise noted), these results show that during the five-year span from 2007 to 2011, private sector satisfaction (including consumers' perceptions regarding a wide variety of common goods and services, but excluding all government services/citizen satisfaction data) averaged between 75.9 and 77.5.[1] These satisfaction scores provide a broad,

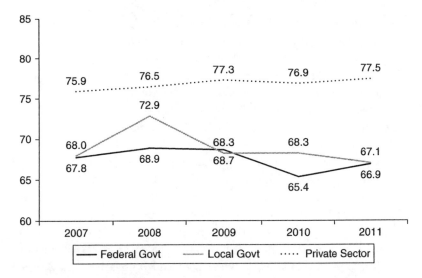

Figure 6.1 Federal government, local government, and private sector satisfaction.
Source: American Customer Satisfaction Index.

general baseline for understanding "average satisfaction" among American consumers with their private sector consumption experiences, and include perceptions of a wide range of goods and services, everything from durable manufactured goods (like automobiles and PCs), to nondurable goods (shampoo and soda), to services (commercial banks and restaurants).

Over this same period, on the other hand, nationwide satisfaction with local government services averaged between 67.1 and 72.9, while satisfaction with federal government agencies ranged between 65.4 and 68.9. The average annual gap between private sector and local government services (the average of the absolute numerical distance between the two measures each year) is nearly 8 points on the 0–100 scale, while the gap between the private sector and federal government is even larger, averaging more than 9 points. Given the amount of data we are working with in this exercise (i.e., tens of thousands of individual respondents, or survey interviews, collected independently each year), these gaps are both very large and highly significant in a statistical sense, suggesting that private sector satisfaction is indeed substantially higher than satisfaction with government services, and is consistently so. Moreover, while not shown here, results from *all* earlier available years of ACSI data and analysis show a pattern and gap nearly identical to this one. But what is the explanation for these large and seemingly persistent gaps?

As we examined to some extent in both chapters 1 and 2, the classic and still most popular explanation for the poorer performance of government vis-à-vis the private sector in providing high-quality, satisfying services to consumers lies in the fact that government lacks competition. The original source for this line of thought is classical economic theory, where consumer interests—in regards to both better prices and higher quality—are thought to be best served by a free, competitive market.[2] But unlike the private sector, where consumers typically have choice among competing suppliers and are able to select freely between those competitors, who in turn attempt to lure consumers with better quality and/or lower prices (or a more diverse group of offerings, new features and innovations, etc.), and where poor-performers are eventually pushed out of the marketplace through this competitive process, in most areas government has no direct competition. Indeed, there certainly appears to be at least some truth to this argument, as even within the private sector there is a fairly clear relationship between the amount of competition within consumer industries and customer satisfaction, with greater competition (or a larger number of alternative suppliers and lower barriers to switching) leading to higher satisfaction, as illustrated in figure 6.2.

As this data shows, for industries where competition is greater, and/or where fewer barriers to switching between suppliers exist, satisfaction tends to be higher. For industries like soft drinks, beer, automobiles, and household appliances, there are many companies competing for customers' dollars and loyalty, and relatively few obstacles to switching to a competitor (like long-term contracts or tangible penalties for switching) that suppliers are able to erect. In turn, strong, above-average satisfaction is the norm for these industries. Comparing these industry-level satisfaction scores with the private sector–only average of 77.5 (from 2011, as all data in the figure reflect 2011 ACSI satisfaction scores), and one can see that each of these industries score more than 3 points above that average (a statistically significant advantage), suggesting that all do a better-than-normal job of satisfying consumers.

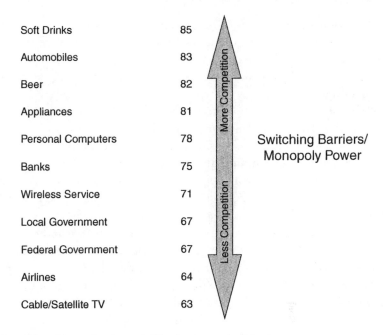

Soft Drinks	85
Automobiles	83
Beer	82
Appliances	81
Personal Computers	78
Banks	75
Wireless Service	71
Local Government	67
Federal Government	67
Airlines	64
Cable/Satellite TV	63

Figure 6.2 Monopoly power, switching barriers, and satisfaction.
Source: American Customer Satisfaction Index, 2011.

On the other hand, looking at industries like personal computers, banks, and wireless telephone service providers, competition certainly does exist in these industries, but the nature of the product/service and the suppliers themselves have created barriers to switching—like the ubiquitous multiyear, penalty-ridden contract forced on consumers by wireless service providers, the location and number of brick-and-mortar branches and ATMs for banks, and the reliance on and familiarity with operating systems and software for PCs—and have thereby diminished choice, with somewhat lower satisfaction (at or well below the private sector average) the consequence. But at the very bottom of the satisfaction spectrum, substantially below the private sector–only average, are government services, where very little or no competition exists, and industries like commercial airlines and cable TV, where competition is significantly limited by nearly monopolistic market conditions (perhaps not coincidentally, monopoly conditions created by government intervention and regulation) and consumers have little or no choice. Thus confirming both intuition and classical economic theory, both consumer utility and satisfaction do indeed appear to be related to competition, perhaps explaining the persistently lagging satisfaction of government services.

What should we make of the free market-citizen satisfaction connection this data shows, and how might it inform efforts to improve satisfaction with government? The most straightforward response to this finding, and a solution that has been popular among academics and politicians alike, is to open-up government services to competition from the private sector wherever possible, to "privatize government," so to speak. And indeed, governments around the world have been increasingly outsourcing many of their traditional areas of authority—including education, prisons, and social service delivery, among many others—to the private sector over the last few decades.[3]

Yet the story may not be as simple as this, and thus solutions more complicated as well. To be sure, while a lack of competition might be an undeniable obstacle to government in providing private-sector-like satisfaction, the *kinds* of services government is required to provide also plays a role. It is hard to imagine, for example, that simply transferring the tax collection responsibility from the IRS to a private company would make it a highly satisfying experience for citizens, nor would most private sector companies even want to manage this "service" to begin with. Furthermore, it is an oversimplification to suggest that each and every government agency provides below average satisfaction, indicating that lack of competition may not entirely explain poor citizen satisfaction, a matter we examine below in lesson #3, following a brief interlude to investigate one additional negative attribute of the satisfaction government provides.

- *Lesson 2*: *Not only does government perform worse on average than the private sector, but it also tends to exhibit greater variance in satisfaction delivery across agencies, programs, and services than the private sector.*

Before we proceed to an example of how some government agencies actually manage to offer strong, even above-average and better-than-the-private-sector satisfaction—a fact that undermines lack of competition as a universally valid and fully sufficient explanation for poor government satisfaction—it is worth noting one additional negative characteristic of government performance: larger inter-agency satisfaction variance, or a larger gap, between the best and worst performers.

To illustrate this phenomenon, we will examine satisfaction across federal government Internet websites (or e-government), a type of service we also discuss in greater detail below. Here we examine a large sample of US federal government website satisfaction scores from 2011. The sample includes data from a total of 315 distinct federal website satisfaction scores, generated through interviews of tens of thousands of actual users of these websites.[4] The websites measured cut across several distinct categories, including employ-ment and career/recruitment sites (such as the Department of Labor and Department of State's career sites), main homepage and portal sites (the main sites for the Centers for Disease Control and the Federal Bureau of Investigation), e-commerce and transactional sites (the application page for the SSA and its benefits programs and the online catalog for the US Mint), and news and information sites (the page for Medline Plus and other health information resources). Table 6.1 provides descriptive statistics for the overall sample of all of the e-government website satisfaction scores measured in 2011, as well as statistics for each distinct federal website category broken-out separately.

As shown in the table, the average satisfaction score across the full sample of e-government website measures is 75.4. This score is reasonably close to the average satisfaction score for all private sector websites measured over the same period (while not included in the table, this score was 77.6 in 2011), indicating that government lags

Table 6.1   E-government website satisfaction

	N	MIN	MAX	MEAN	SD
All E-Government Websites	315	53	91	75.4	7.3
News/Information	161	53	89	74.9	7.3
Main/Portal	99	57	85	74.7	6.4
E-Commerce/Transaction	40	56	91	78.4	9.5
Career/Recruitment	15	69	83	77.3	4.6

the private sector by a fairly small margin. As we saw in lesson #1, for example, this gap is significantly smaller than that found between the private sector and federal or local government overall, suggesting e-government may be a "top performer" among government services and offerings (and may provide some evidence that, at least in this one area, government need not lag the private sector by a large margin in satisfying consumers, a matter we expand on in the next lesson).

On the other hand, this data also shows that satisfaction is not constant across the various categories of e-government sites. E-commerce/transactional websites score highest at 78.4, a score even better than the overall private sector average, while main/portal sites score lowest at 74.7, with a gap of 3.7 points separating the two categories. More important, though, is the substantial range of 38 points between the lowest scoring ("MIN"=53) and the highest scoring ("MAX"=91) websites among the full sample of e-government sites. The comparable range is only 20 points for the private sector (from 66.0 to 86.0), indicating a far smaller gap between best- and worst-performing private sector websites. In other words, it appears that e-government is not being implemented equally well—at least in the minds of users of these sites—across all federal government agencies, and particularly when compared to the private sector. While some websites are performing at an extremely high level in satisfying users, on par with or even better than the private sector, some perform much worse in terms of user satisfaction, scoring even as low as the low 50s (a score similar to the all-time-worst score in ACSI for any private sector measure). This finding suggests that there remains significant variation in user satisfaction with e-government sites, much more variance than one finds in the private sector.

The example of e-government/website satisfaction touches on an important lesson about government satisfaction performance, a lesson that transcends one particular point in time or channel of service delivery. While these results show that the type of service or function being offered by an e-government site matters in terms of user satisfaction (a vital issue we return to below), with some performing better on average (e-commerce/transactional websites) than others (main/portal websites) based on the nature of their task or mission, it also highlights that in the eyes of citizens, government performance is often all over the proverbial map.[5] Consistency in delivering satisfaction seems to elude government across its parts, while private sector companies tend to converge and offer very similar consumer satisfaction (or at least less variance in satisfaction). So why do distinct governments units—whether departments, agencies, or some other discrete service-offering unit—tend to vary more than comparable private sector organizations do in providing citizen satisfaction? Some explanations for this phenomenon exist.

One likely and convincing explanation for the disparate performance across government agencies in offering a satisfying experience is the availability of financial resources, with some programs having far less resources to devote to providing high-quality services, and others better able to do so. In the example provided above, for instance, it is undoubtedly the case that some agencies and departments are in a more advantageous financial position to focus resources on the creation of high-quality, user-friendly websites than others, precisely because these organizations are given more financial resources by the political system to do so. In short, given that some agencies can gain access to resources and truly devote attention and effort to provide a state-of-the-art online experience, while others must make do with less, the range in performance is understandable.

Another explanation may lie in the exclusive jurisdiction and resulting "functional silos" that exist between distinct government agencies and departments. The autonomy provided to most government departments (a by-product of the American checks and balances/separation of powers principle) has often been regarded as a detriment to integration or homogenization across agencies and programs of all kinds, often resulting in stark differences in how agencies interact with the public at large and deliver services.[6] But regardless of the reason, government services tend to vary more than the private sector, as this example shows, and this fact means citizens will likely continue to receive disparate levels of satisfaction depending on the government unit providing the service. And assuming that the factors causing this situation will not vanish overnight, it is likely that this variance will continue to prove an impediment for government in providing better, consistent, and strong aggregate citizen satisfaction in the future.

- *Lesson #3: These negative characteristics aside, not all government programs and agencies perform poorly, and some even perform as well as or better than comparable private sector services in delivering satisfaction.*

If competition (or a lack thereof) is indeed a fully sufficient explanation for poor government satisfaction performance when compared to the private sector, as is often suggested and at least partially confirmed by the evidence presented in lesson #1 above, then one would expect this explanation to apply universally. That is, if this factor is enough in and of itself to explain lower citizen satisfaction, then wherever government has little or no competition (i.e., in virtually every instance), it should be the case that low satisfaction is observable. In turn, such a finding would certainly confirm and support political prescriptions for improving government through the introduction of market-like management reforms and private sector practices—and perhaps even some privatization of government services—throughout government, a recommendation that has been popular (and gaining in popularity) over the last few decades.[7] Yet this does not appear to be true. As the case of the Veterans Health Administration (VHA) and its satisfaction performance shows, government is capable of providing satisfaction to its users that rivals and even surpasses comparable services from the private sector. First, consider figure 6.3.

Figure 6.3 shows satisfaction with private sector hospitals, along with satisfaction for both the VHA's inpatient and its outpatient services separately, between 2007 and 2011.[8] As these results show, not only did the VHA provide satisfaction to its patients that matches the private sector, but over these years both inpatient and outpatient satisfaction with VHA's services significantly exceeded that for private sector hospitals. While a skeptic might claim that the VHA does have competition—in the form of private sector hospitals that veterans could always turn to if they wanted to refuse VHA's services—the sheer number and proportion of veterans who use its specialized services (more than eight million each year according to the VA), the complexity and unique nature of many of the services offered by VHA, and the expenses that would be required of veterans if they chose the private sector alternative (in other words, many veterans don't really have a choice for practical financial reasons),

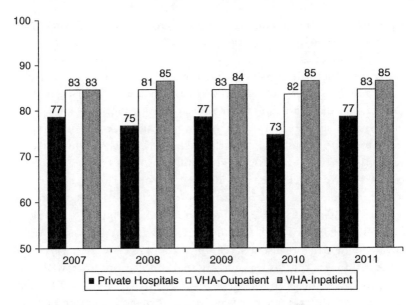

Figure 6.3 VHA versus private hospital satisfaction.
Source: American Customer Satisfaction Index.

belie this counterclaim. Moreover, while the existence of competition could explain *comparable* or even performance for the two types of hospitals, it would not explain why VHA *exceeds* the private sector in terms of satisfaction. In short, the idea that satisfaction with government is always, unequivocally below the private sector, because of lack of competition or based on any other explanation, does not appear to be defensible.[9]

So if a lack of competition cannot be employed to explain the lower satisfaction provided by government when compared to the private sector, at least not in every case without exception, then what does explain this phenomenon? At least to some extent, I would argue, the nature of the jobs government agencies are tasked with performing (or in the language of government, their mission) is a likely explanation for the poor performance of government in many or even most cases. After all, while government may not provide as much satisfaction as the private sector, it is also inarguable that the private sector generally does not perform tasks as inherently displeasing as many of those performed by the IRS (coercively taking citizens' money), the

TSA (invasively inspecting traveling passengers), or most other agencies with primarily regulatory missions. And as long as government is the authority tasked with these jobs, it is likely to continue to lag the private sector in satisfying consumers, at least in the aggregate.

In general, at least based on satisfaction data and our interpretation of that data, proclamations that government should simply "be more like the private sector" toward improving citizen satisfaction are too simplistic. These often overlook the fact that government does very different and intrinsically difficult jobs, jobs few private sector companies would choose to do if given the opportunity, and in fact it does other things quite well. As shown above with the case of the VHA, and with services like those provided by the NPS examined in the last chapter (which was shown to provide strong satisfaction), government can provide a satisfying experience to citizen-users in some instances. Yet this is not to say that innovations borrowed from the private sector cannot help government do a better job. Indeed, in lesson #5 we examine one way government has integrated private sector technologies quite effectively, and improved citizen satisfaction as a consequence.

- *Lesson #4: Citizens come to their encounters with government expecting much less than they expect from the private sector, with negative consequences for citizen satisfaction.*

Similar to lesson #1 above, the claim that citizens tend to expect less (that is to say, have significantly lower prior expectations) about their experiences with government before those experiences occur than they do with the private sector should come as little surprise. Given the "negative buzz" surrounding many or even most experiences with government (of all types and at all levels), negative buzz created by an almost never-ending barrage of attacks on government institutions from virtually all quarters, it is perhaps more surprising that citizens expect anything positive whatsoever. Furthermore, relating this claim to the discussion in lesson #3, greater variance across government agencies or programs may also make it hard for citizens to develop realistically positive expectations with government, as they never know what they might receive from one experience

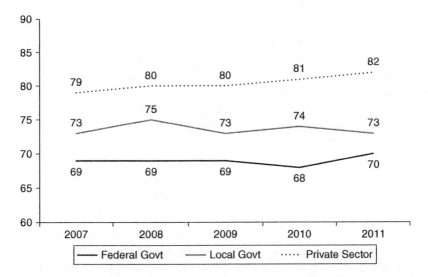

Figure 6.4 Federal government, local government, and private sector expectations.
Source: American Customer Satisfaction Index.

to the next. Yet regardless of the cause, the consequences of these deflated expectations are different and more impactful than most understand. First, consider figure 6.4, which compares government and private sector consumers' expectations.

Again using a 0–100 scale, but this time examining pre-experience expectations for both the public (federal and local government) and the private sectors (again excluding all government/citizen satisfaction data) rather than postexperience satisfaction, one can see the large gap in expectations that separates them. On average across the five years of data shown here, citizen expectations with federal government are more than 11 points lower than expectations in the private sector, a large and highly statistically significant difference. Similarly, citizen expectations with local government, while significantly higher than expectations with federal government, are nearly 7 points lower on average than the private sector. In short, these results show that citizens are far less predisposed to anticipate high-quality services from their government experiences prior to those experiences than they are from the private sector, believing rather that they'll get less satisfaction from the government.

But are the lower expectations citizens have with government services a good or a bad thing? While it might be nice for citizens to expect the world from government, perhaps these low expectations are not so bad. Indeed, an argument can be (and occasionally is) made that depressed expectations are actually *beneficial* to government or other companies and organizations in terms of satisfying their customers. After all, if expectations with government are as depressed as the data shown above indicates, shouldn't government agencies have a much easier time *exceeding* those expectations, and thereby pleasantly surprising the citizen-customers they come into contact with in a manner conducive to higher satisfaction? Don't low expectations make the government's job easier, in a sense? Unfortunately, for most organizations with low expectations this is not the case, and in fact a large body of research into what is known as the expectancy-disconfirmation model has shown that depressed expectations actually have a negative impact on satisfaction across economic sectors.

In abbreviated form, the expectancy-disconfirmation model attempts to clarify the role of a consumer's prior expectations in the processes through which satisfaction judgments regarding some and potentially any experience are formed. The central idea of the model is that there exists a dynamic linkage between expectations, disconfirmation of expectations—including both "positive disconfirmation," implying better-than-expected performance, and "negative disconfirmation," implying worse-than-expected performance—and the satisfaction received from an experience. And what studies of this model have overwhelmingly shown (especially in the context of the public sector) is that those with lower expectations are not more likely to see those expectations positively disconfirmed or exceeded, but rather that consumers generally "get what they expect" in terms of satisfaction, that expectations are most often confirmed through actual experiences.[10] In other words, depressed expectations tend to result in *lower* satisfaction, not greater delight and higher satisfaction.

Taken together, what we can glean from these findings is that deflated expectations actually function to depress satisfaction with government further, and are likely to do so as long as government remains a target of internal and external forces that depress expectations. Moreover, unlike in the private sector, where companies have the resources and wherewithal to perform actions that can raise expectations to higher, more positive levels (like advertising, media campaigns, public relations, and other communications strategies), government is much more limited in its ability to do so, making this "expectations problem" difficult to proactively address. In sum, these low expectations present an additional obstacle to government in overcoming low citizen satisfaction, and this is likely to remain the case in the future.

- *Lesson #5: E-government has been a consistent bright spot for government for nearly a decade, an area where government performance compares more favorably to the private sector.*

The emergence of electronic government (typically referred to by its abbreviated name, "e-government") over the last two decades or so has dramatically altered the way citizens and governments communicate, and the ways in which government offers services to citizens. This transformation has impacted all levels of government, and virtually every government around the world, developed and developing alike. Over the past two decades in the United States, for example, the federal government has integrated e-government into nearly all of the services it offers to citizens. Americans can now receive from the federal government through the Internet and its websites (the most common form of e-government) a truly massive assortment of services (or "e-services"). In addition, virtually every government in the world now has an e-government presence, with some nations (such as South Korea and the Netherlands) boasting systems even better developed, at least by some measures, than those in the United States.[11]

At this point, it would be difficult to overstate the significance of the dawn of the age of e-government, and the changes this technological innovation has ushered in. In part, the move by governments towards delivering services electronically has been guided by a desire to save money; the US federal government has, for example, been estimated to save hundreds of millions of dollars annually due to the adoption of e-government services.[12] Yet cost saving is not the only justification for this move, as a number of other benefits of this new technology have also been suggested. Most importantly, e-government has been viewed as an effective vehicle for government in improving the quality of services delivered to citizens, and through that to enhance citizen satisfaction—and possibly even to provide service quality and satisfaction on par with the private sector. This latter goal is also being achieved, or very nearly so it would seem, as the results in figure 6.5 suggest.

The results in the figure show satisfaction with the private sector–only, with the federal government overall, and with federal e-government websites from 2007 to 2011.[13] And as these numbers show, federal e-government comes much closer to matching the performance of the private sector than does the federal government as a whole. The average annual gap between the private sector overall and federal e-government websites (just as earlier, expressed as the average of the numerical distance between the two measures each year) is just over two points on the 0–100 scale, while the gap between the private sector and federal government overall averages more than 9 points. In short, the move towards e-government on the grounds that it provides better, more satisfying services would seem to be confirmed.

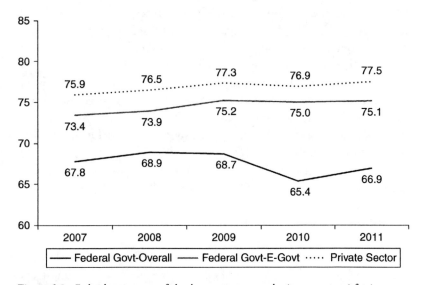

Figure 6.5   Federal government, federal e-government, and private sector satisfaction.
Source: American Customer Satisfaction Index.

But why are federal e-government websites outperforming federal services overall, and in fact nearly matching private sector satisfaction, and what can this finding teach government about improving its citizen satisfaction? In part, these findings speak to the nature of IT itself, and how IT provides a means through which virtually any organization can perform better through the adoption of more user-friendly tools. As satisfaction with private sector websites is often found to exceed other private sector services (as exemplified in the exceptional performance of Amazon.com and similar "e-tailers," and the dramatic decline of print newspapers in the face of Internet news sources), so too does it appear that government IT outperforms traditional government services. Moreover, e-government seems to have leveled the playing field for government to some extent, allowing agencies to develop platforms that are at least comparable to the private sector. Whereas government can rarely compete with the private sector in terms of general customer service offerings based on budgetary and other financial limitations, it can at least come closer to parity in its IT offerings. Finally, it should be remembered here that while researchers often go looking for major problem areas to address in improving satisfaction, in the public as well as the private sectors, sometimes changing relatively little things can have a major impact. As this e-government example shows, satisfaction can oftentimes be improved by simply identifying one vehicle for providing customer service that outperforms others, and then encouraging (or even forcing) customers to adopt the more satisfying vehicle.

Yet a word of caution should be noted. Some analysis has found that there remains room for improvement in e-government offerings, with studies showing that federal e-government does not yet provide satisfaction on par with the most directly comparably private sector alternative, private sector e-business and e-commerce websites,[14] and government has experienced some very high-profile failures in its IT offerings as well.[15] These results suggest that while government does indeed offer more satisfaction online than off-line, it still does not offer services on par with companies like Amazon.com and other major Internet players. Thus while e-government serves as a "bright spot" in terms of citizen satisfaction, more works needs to be done, work that can be accomplished in part through careful measurement and monitoring of citizen experiences with these technologies.

- *Lesson #6: Complaint rates with the government are low, government tends to handle complaints poorly, and together these two factors depress citizen satisfaction in multiple ways.*

In chapter 2 we described the "exit-voice-loyalty" mechanism that helps explain customer or member behavior for most organizations, and specifically how customers of companies in the private sector tend to express dissatisfaction through either formally complaining as their satisfaction declines (using their "voice"), or by "exiting" the organization in search of an alternative, more satisfying supplier. In other words, unhappy consumers tend to either grow more likely to voice their displeasure with a company, or to just leave it altogether. However, we also showed in chapter 2 how this mechanism does not work, or at least not nearly as well, vis-à-vis satisfaction with monopolistic government organizations and their services. The figure provided in chapter 2, and reproduced below (see figure 6.6), shows that while customer satisfaction and the rate at which customers complain tend to be inversely related for private sector companies (i.e., as satisfaction drops, complaints rise), the same does not hold for government:

While in chapter 2 we discussed the phenomenon of low complaint rate with government services in general, and how satisfaction measurement might potentially provide a new network of communication for better connecting state and society absent interaction through complaints, what we have not considered is why so few customers complain to government, the (negative) consequences of this lack of complaining for these organizations, and especially the impact of this tendency on government agencies' ability to improve citizen satisfaction.

While many might be proffered, perhaps the most convincing explanation for why customers fail to complain when dissatisfied with their government experiences relates to the economic principle of return on investment. Put simply, return on investment measures the difference between what you put in and what you get back, or the positive gain one can expect from performing some action (or buying a stock, lending someone money, etc.). Whereas in the private sector many consumers are apt to complain when they feel they have been mistreated (i.e., when they are dissatisfied), most do so in

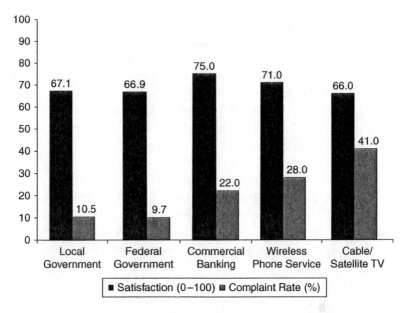

Figure 6.6 Complaint rates and satisfaction across economic sectors.
Source: American Customer Satisfaction Index, 2011.

the hope that the act of complaining will itself result in some kind of *positive* return on investment, that they'll get from this act more than they put in. In this instance, the thing being "invested" through complaint behavior is primarily the consumer's time. The positive expected return for the consumer might include a refund or replacement of a faulty product, a discount on future purchases, or even the psychological pleasure received through an official apology from the company. Yet citizens don't seem to feel the same way about government, as evidenced by the low complaint rate, instead believing that the act of complaining would itself constitute a further time expenditure with a limited or null return; in other words, citizens feel they are unlikely to get anything positive by complaining to government about bad experiences, so they refrain from complaining altogether.

What leads to this pessimistic assessment among citizens about a return on investment when complaining to government? It seems likely that some of this pessimism stems from the low expectations citizens have of government experiences mentioned earlier. Another related explanation might be found in low general trust in government, a matter we turn to next and close the chapter with. But in terms of empirical data, the poor manner in which government agencies handle or respond to complaints seems to offer a compelling explanation for why so few citizens complain to government in the first place. Figure 6.7 provides scores for complaint handling (on a 0–100 scale) for both the government and selected private sector industries, and shows complaint handling to be a weak spot for government, as well as a strong possible explanation for why citizens complain infrequently.

Thus while other explanations for citizens' relatively low rate of complaint to government about dissatisfying experiences exist, the poor manner in which government handles the complaints of those citizens who do complain—a score lower than virtually all industries in the private sector, and as bad as the complaint handling practices of the airlines, one of the private sector's most dissatisfying industries—is certainly one.

But is this low complaint rate really a bad situation for government? Shouldn't government officials instead be happy that relatively few citizens complain, given that fielding and managing complaints

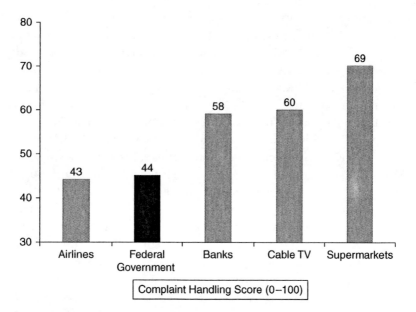

Figure 6.7 Complaint handling across economic sectors.
Source: American Customer Satisfaction Index, 2011.

takes time, effort, and resources, even if they are managed poorly? Indeed, doesn't it at least seem like many private sector companies make it as hard as possible to complain, making the low government complaint phenomenon enviable by comparison?[16] Yet while some might see a silver lining in this low complaint rate, it is in fact not a positive characteristic, for at least two reasons.

First, while managing and fielding complaints may require some resource expenditure for government agencies or any other organization, it also presents an opportunity for government to turn dissatisfied citizens into satisfied ones. Figure 6.8 shows federal government citizen satisfaction scores for complaining customers broken into two groups—those who felt their complaint was handled well, and those who thought it was handled poorly. And as this data shows, citizens who complained but felt their complaint was well-handled are dramatically more satisfied (a score of 65) than those who felt their complaint was handled poorly (a score of only 25). In short, what this data shows is that, if done well, a well-managed complaint can convert an unhappy citizen into at least a moderately happy one. And when the dissatisfied citizen refuses to

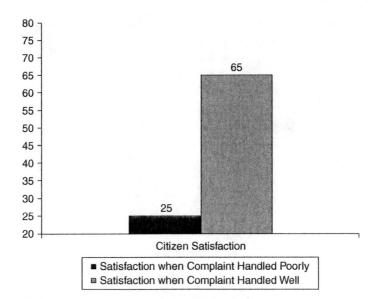

Figure 6.8   Citizen satisfaction and complaint handling.
Source: American Customer Satisfaction Index.

complain altogether, the possibility of turning a dissatisfied citizen into a satisfied one is lost.

Secondly, complaints, if managed and monitored appropriately, can provide a wealth of information to an organization that can help it improve its performance, not just with a single complaining consumer, but in the aggregate. That is, receiving complaints from customers gives the organization a unique ability to learn about the sources of consumer dissatisfaction directly, from the "horse's mouth," as it were. This kind of information, if collected properly—perhaps through one of the growing number of complaint management software systems that allow CSRs to record the nature and cause of the complaint—and analyzed correctly, can actually replace or at least augment more expensive research into citizen experiences.

The bottom line for government is that citizens don't complain and prefer to stew in their dissatisfaction, leading to lingering negative feelings about government and, as we saw earlier, depressed expectations about what they will receive in future encounters. This fact both prevents government from mending dissatisfaction for the individual citizen, and likewise prevents it from collecting valuable information about poor processes and services over the long run, information that could help improve experiences and aggregate satisfaction. One solution to this problem is to find ways to get citizens to complain, to actually attempt to "maximize complaints" and glean valuable information that may help improve processes and services in the future. And a promising avenue for complaint maximization has recently emerged; through social media and other recent IT innovations, convenient, easy-to-use, and inexpensive platforms now exist that can help government encourage citizens to voice their dissatisfaction and its causes.

- *Lesson #7: Citizen satisfaction has a positive impact on citizen trust in government, both trust in the government overall and in particular government agencies. Improving citizen satisfaction provides an ideal (and realistic) strategy for improving lagging trust in government.*

Most American citizens have very little trust in the US federal government. With just a few fleeting exceptions, this statement has been true since the early 1970s. According to research from the Pew Center based on an analysis of multiple long-running surveys dating back to the 1950s, the percentage of citizens that trust the government—defined as those Americans who indicate that they "trust the government in Washington most of the time" or "all of the time"—declined from 73 percent in 1958 to only around 25 percent in 1980. After improving briefly in the mid 1980s and slowly but consistently throughout the 1990s and early 2000s to around 55 percent, the number plummeted to only 19 percent by 2010.[17] While the politically turbulent years from 2002 to 2010—marked by wars, economic turmoil, mounting government debt and politically contentious responses to that debt, and so forth—certainly did nothing to improve the situation, low and/or declining citizen trust in government has been a problem plaguing the American federal system and political administrations of all types for more than four decades.

As we discussed in chapter 2, fostering trust in government is more than an academic concern, and few would deny its import. Indeed, there are a variety of benefits often connected to improved trust in government, including enhanced cooperation between state and society, a lessened need for a coercive regulatory environment through increased voluntary compliance by citizens, and so forth. Overall, a political system that enjoys the trust of its citizenry is more likely to be a stable political system made-up of contented citizens, a political system with an easier job governing society. But the question of *how* trust in government can be restored is a difficult one, a dilemma that rests in a web of definitions of what trust is, how it is lost, and how it can be reproduced.[18]

Competing explanations for why American citizens (in particular) have come to trust government less and less point at somewhat different underlying causes. The first and most obvious explanation relates to the seemingly endless cycle of major political scandals that began in the 1960s—Vietnam, Watergate, Iran-Contra, Monica Lewinsky, and so forth. As citizen trust began to decline rapidly at about the same time and has remained mostly low since, these scandals make an easy and convincing culprit. Moreover, both academic research and an abundance of popular commentary have suggested that growing political partisanship and a deepening divide between parties and ideologies have caused Americans to distrust government, no matter which "side" is in power.[19] Other research has pointed to a general decline in civic association and a loss of "social capital" in the United States (and Western democracies in general), exemplified in the "bowling alone" hypothesis advanced by Robert Putnam, as being responsible for a decline in both interpersonal trust and citizen trust toward political institutions.[20] Some have even suggested that government itself is to blame for the declining trust it has experienced, and this applies to most governments the world over. As nation-states assumed greater and greater authority over a larger number of activities that impact citizens' lives throughout the twentieth century, through the advent and expansion of the social welfare state, it also unwittingly assumed greater responsibility for the inevitable failures that plague those lives.[21] Under such circumstances, whenever virtually anything goes wrong it can be perceived as a symptom of "bad government," according to this hypothesis.

Yet while the sources of growing distrust in government can be debated, along with the various possible solutions depending upon the differential diagnoses of the problem, most would agree that one major source of declining trust—and one that is not necessarily contradictory to any of the alternative explanations mentioned above, and quite possibly intertwined with them all—lies in increasingly negative perceptions of actual government performance. More specifically, citizens' perceptions that government does a poor, low-quality, and inefficient job delivering services likely helps explain declining trust in government, and thus improving both actual performance and citizen perceptions of and satisfaction with that performance serves as a means for counteracting declining trust. And viewing the trust issue from this perspective, citizen satisfaction measurement can certainly help both diagnose the sources of perceptions of poor performance, as we have described in several of the preceding chapters, while also defining strategies for improving both satisfaction and trust in government. Moreover, it can be argued that satisfaction measurement and reforms and improvements based on this data provide a solution to the trust problem most open to real, direct action; unlike practical action derived from satisfaction measurement and process improvements, stopping political scandals, reversing partisanship, reinvigorating social capital or rolling-back the welfare state are all "big problems" requiring "big solutions" and dramatic, even revolutionary action.

In chapters 4 and 5, we provided empirical evidence of the strong link between citizen satisfaction and both confidence in particular government agencies and overall trust in the federal government, and it is unnecessary to reiterate those findings in detail here. But going beyond these results and looking at the same data over a number of years (instead of aggregated into a single model as we did in the earlier chapters), in figure 6.9 we see that satisfaction and measures of trust move together not only within a single data set (i.e., cross-sectionally), but also in the aggregate over time (i.e., longitudinally). Once again, as was the case in the model results in chapter 4, a clearer and stronger relationship exists between satisfaction and confidence in the agency over time, than between satisfaction and overall trust in government over time. This is most likely due to the way these two variables are measured (with trust being a much more abstract entity), but also speaks to a dynamic lagged relationship between satisfaction, confidence in an agency, and overall trust in government. That is, as satisfaction increases confidence in the

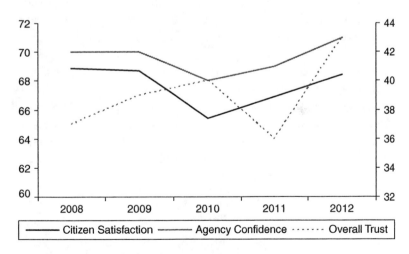

Figure 6.9 Citizen satisfaction, trust, and confidence over time.
Source: American Customer Satisfaction Index.

agency increases both contemporaneously and in the future, and in combination these two factors lead to a future increase in overall trust in government.

To be clear, and perhaps anticipate objections, we are not claiming here that citizen satisfaction is the only or even necessarily the primary cause (or influencing factor) driving confidence or overall trust in government; as any data researcher will tell you, correlation alone does not prove causation. Moreover, as other researchers have pointed out, it is possibly the case that there exists no simple direct relationship between satisfaction and trust, or between any single variable and trust. Rather, it is more likely the case that a dynamic relationship exists, and possibly even a circular relationship: poor performance diminishes satisfaction and trust, which in turn diminish perceptions of (and expectations with) performance in the future, which more deeply diminishes trust, and so on.[22] But again, we need not believe that satisfaction is the only and exclusive explanation for or solution to declining trust to identify it as an important one, and a path that is perhaps more "fixable" than some of the others.

Thus while satisfaction is not a panacea in terms of reversing the decline in citizen trust, aiming for improved citizen satisfaction through better government performance and improved services provides one practical reform opportunity for government to have an active and positive impact on diminished trust. Regardless of how the downward spiral in trust actually began, government can and should take an active role in mending this problem, and satisfaction measurement and improvement strategies can help in these efforts. And as we will discuss in the next and final chapter, feasible and cost-effective strategies for improving both satisfaction and citizen trust are likely to become more vital than ever before, as the world appears to be entering a phase where governments will be forced to serve more citizens with fewer resources.

Conclusion

This chapter has attempted to provide insights into a diverse assortment of findings regarding citizen satisfaction and related metrics. Because these findings have recurred so regularly over the years and across various samples of data collected via surveys of citizens, they represent something approaching concrete truths. And as such, they are intended to provide insight into likely findings from similar studies in the future and across contexts, findings that hold over time and across levels of government, and possibly even across national and political contexts as well.

CHAPTER 7

Governing in an Age of Scarcity: On the Role of Cross-National Citizen Satisfaction Measurement

Introduction

In this chapter, we begin by examining a series of global changes and challenges that, in our estimation, significantly increase the importance of citizen satisfaction measurement (and of performance measurement in general) as a vital tool for governments seeking to most efficiently allocate scarce resources, and for improving citizens' satisfaction and trust in government in the process. As the global population continues to both rise and age over the next century (perhaps dramatically so), and as budgetary resources likely become less plentiful, at least on a per-working-citizen basis, governments must respond by maximizing the resources they have in a manner that best meets citizen wants and needs. While obviously an extreme scenario, and one that may seem (at least superficially) only tangentially related to citizen satisfaction measurement, a review of the recent (2010 to present) political upheavals in North Africa and the Middle East known collectively as the "Arab Spring," along with similar instances of unrest in places like Greece and Spain, help to clarify the dangers governments can experience under the difficult circumstance where they are forced to "serve more with less." In the end, we propose and briefly outline a global system of citizen satisfaction measurement useful for benchmarking and sharing best practices across disparate national governments, a tool that can help these governments effectively use their resources in a manner most beneficial to both citizen satisfaction and citizen trust.

The Challenges Ahead

A Sign of the Times?

In December of 2010, a series of uprisings began that would rock the nations of North Africa and the Middle East over the ensuing months and years. Beginning in the unlikely nation of Tunisia—a geographically smaller, less populous country where, at least by North African standards, citizens enjoyed a relatively high standard of living and more expansive personal freedoms—the protests, riots, and in some cases outright revolutions sparked by the "Jasmine Revolution" spread to nations like Egypt, Libya, Saudi Arabia, and Syria, among several others. Known collectively as the "Arab Spring," the series of interconnected events that took shape during this period (and that continued to unfold as of this writing, in fact, most notably in Syria and Lebanon) fundamentally reshaped the political dynamic of the Arab world, and the still-uncertain ramifications of these changes will likely be felt for many decades to come.[1]

For some good reasons, the dominant narrative in the West surrounding the events of the Arab Spring has focused on a backlash against authoritarianism, dictatorship, historical injustice, and political corruption, and in many ways this perspective is accurate. In virtually all of the states where the instability of the Arab Spring became manifest, the governments in charge had a long history of undemocratic, absolutist rule that siphoned money from the public treasuries and abused or entirely rejected the fundamental rights of citizens. Prior to the Arab Spring, the governments in this region boasted some of the longest running and richest "presidents" in the world, such as Hosni Mubarak in Egypt (1981–2011) and Muammar Gaddafi in Libya (1969–2011).[2] Therefore, the notion that these revolts emerged in these particular states at this specific moment in time as a direct consequence of decades of pent-up rage and frustration with corrupt, undemocratic rule is certainly plausible, at least in part.

But as others have pointed out, equally accurately, the political conditions often identified as the primary cause of the Arab Spring had existed for years, and even multiple decades in most of these countries, prior to the outbreak of unrest. Moreover, many of these countries had seen a significant (albeit gradual) increase in their standard of living and the government's distribution of social goods like education, health care, employment opportunities, and so forth, in the decades prior to the Arab Spring. Thus, focusing exclusively on the historical abuses of the regimes in this region likely does not tell the entire story of what inspired the Arab Spring.

Yet if these uprisings cannot be blamed exclusively on these most visible and well-referenced factors, at least not as the sole and exclusive causes, why did they occur when they did and not, say, ten years earlier or later? While clearly not as "sexy" or open to quick, media-friendly interpretations, there are several additional and interconnected factors that help explain the timing of the Arab Spring that deserve consideration, factors that are directly related to many of the ideas we have discussed thus far in this text. Two such factors are the culmination of a long period of population growth in the Arab countries, and governmental budget constraints resulting from the global recession of 2008–2009.[3]

First, let's very briefly consider population growth in North Africa—where the Arab Spring uprisings began—between 1950 and 2010, as shown in the figure below:

As shown in figure 7.1, between 1950 and 2010 the population of North Africa grew from just over 50 million people to more than 200 million, astounding growth of almost 300 percent over the period.

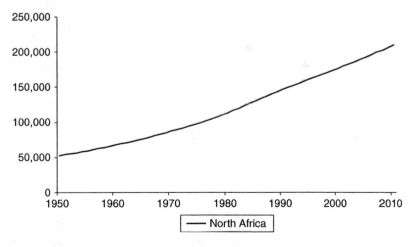

Figure 7.1 Population growth in North Africa: 1950–2010.

By comparison, the US population grew about 97 percent over the same period, while Europe saw growth of only around 34 percent. In some of the Arab states mentioned earlier, Tunisia, Egypt, and Libya, the countries where the Arab Spring began and was felt most powerfully, population growth was very significant as well, with Tunisia seeing growth of about 197 percent, Egypt with 277 percent growth, and Libya with an enormous 518 percent growth. In short, both the overall region (as well as the broader Middle East) and most of the individual countries in the region that felt the effects of the Arab Spring were at the end of an era of very substantial population growth, far greater than many/ most other regions in the world, and certainly more dramatic than in the more developed states of Europe and North America.

In addition to this long period of dramatic population growth, the societies of North Africa and the Middle East had experienced economic and government budget turmoil coupled with rapidly rising prices throughout the 2000s (even preceding the Great Recession that began in late 2008) that put a great strain on the living standards of their populations. Throughout the early 2000s, riots had intermittently impacted many of the nations in the region. These rioters protested against dramatic price increases (even in basic goods like flour—which is a major issue for Egyptians, for instance, who are the world's largest per-capita consumers of bread), a lack of employment opportunities for the large and growing number of young, college-educated people entering the workforce, a lack of adequate housing and other basic goods, inadequate wages and/or working conditions, and so forth. Only exacerbated by the free flow of information made possible by the advent of social media and other IT innovations, the early 2000s were marked by a period of growing unrest across much of the Arab world.

Yet for many of the governments in this region, real trouble only began in the fall of 2008. While much has been said about the underlying causes and short- and long-term consequences of the global Great Recession, its impacts were undeniable and most stark on the regimes of North Africa and the Middle East. While the price of oil had been historically high for most of the 2000s prior to late 2008, thereby providing enormous wealth for the many oil-rich Arab states,[4] the impact of the recession on this already inflation-squeezed and resource-limited region were dramatic. The governments in this region, most of which exercise (or exercised) extraordinary authority over society, yet as a consequence shouldered an enormous burden for any perceived failures in providing services to citizens, lost the ability (i.e., the available budgetary resources) to adequately cushion the economic blow of the recession and to continue to offer services that citizens (and a larger number of citizens at that) had come to depend upon. In short, while virtually every country in the world felt the economic effects of the 2008–2009 recession, many of the Arab states felt the pinch particularly strongly, and this manifest itself in a *perception among the population that these governments were performing poorly*, even by their own, somewhat lower standards.[5]

One final thing to note. While there were many causes driving the Arab Spring, it has been forgotten in many quarters that the immediate event inspiring these revolts were the desperate actions of one man—one man in a dispute with an inefficient, corrupt bureaucracy over a simple state-issued license. In a sense, rather than some "final insult" of massive political corruption or rights abuses, the Arab Spring was caused by the self-immolation of a man named Mohamed Bouazizi in December of 2010, an act that came on the heels of a disagreement between Bouazizi and local government officials in his home town over a permit to sell fruit. Like many in the countries of North Africa, Bouazizi was underemployed, and earned his living buying (on credit) and selling produce from a cart. After having his cart and all of its contents confiscated by police for lack of a permit—which, in fact, wasn't really needed—and appealing to more senior bureaucrats to have his cart and wares returned, who chose to only insult and humiliate him further, Bouazizi could take no more, and on the morning of December 17 he protested this abuse by dousing himself in gasoline and setting himself on fire. Bouazizi died on January 4, 2011, and his actions, word of which spread throughout the region very rapidly via social media and the Internet, became the rallying cry for young Arabs across North Africa and the Middle East. In a sense, then, it is correct to say that the immediate cause of the Arab Spring was a dispute between a man and a government bureaucracy, a direct consequence of *massive displeasure (dissatisfaction) with a corrupt bureaucratic system*.

This quick review of the events surrounding the Arab Spring is not intended to make the dubious claim that, somehow, in some way, performance measurement or citizen satisfaction measurement alone could have (or even should have) prevented this historically significant moment. This historic series of events was driven by a complex confluence of causes cultural, social, economic, political, and governmental. But certainly one central cause in all of this was centered in *government performance and citizen perceptions of poor performance* under difficult conditions, with large and growing populations expecting their governments to provide high-quality, efficient, and needed services to the population, and with the governments failing to do so effectively under these stressful conditions. What is more, certain aspects of these events highlight in a clear way, I would argue, the unique difficulties that are *very likely to lie ahead for governments around the world*. In turn, they also help clarify the role that performance measurement absolutely must play as governments try to contend with these conditions. A brief review of the coming changes to the global population and global resources will help illustrate these challenges.

The Coming Population and Budget Crunch

Between 2010 and 2100, it is predicted that the population of the world will grow substantially. While the precision of these predictions is less than perfect, virtually no one disputes their essence—the population of the world is poised to jump much higher over the next 90 years. Figure 7.2 provides the UN's "medium" and "high" estimates of global population growth between the years 2010 and 2100.

Based on these UN estimates, the global population is set to grow by between a little more than 3 billion to as many as 9 billion more people by the year 2100, from a total global population of around 7 billion people today to a population somewhere between *10 and 16 billion people*. Many individual countries, even already-developed, resource-rich countries, are projected to grow substantially over this period as well. The United States, for example, is projected to add between 160 million to as many as *400 million new citizens*, for a total population of between 480 and 700 million people, by the year

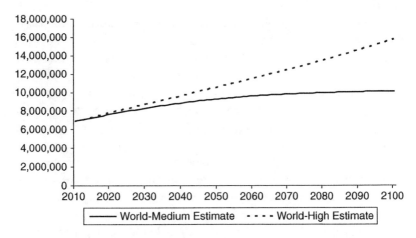

Figure 7.2   UN world population growth estimates: 2010–2100.

2100.[6] In short, for many governments across the globe, both small and large, wealthy and poor, developed and developing, the number of citizens they are going to be expected to serve is set to increase significantly in the twenty-first century.

In addition to this growing population, governments around the world have been taking on more debt over the past decade than at any point in history (or at least since the turbulent days of the first half of the twentieth century), and high national debt-to-GDP ratios (the amount of government debt relative to total national economic output) are only expected to grow in the years ahead, with increasingly higher levels of debt being added relative to economic growth. While some of this debt has been accumulated only recently to deal with the effects of the global recession,[7] there are changes that have been occurring in many societies—changes related to the added government capacity needed to manage the population growth discussed above—that suggest government debt problems are likely to remain significant or even worsen substantially, even in the event of a significant and unexpected economic boom (such as the one that followed World War II) in the coming decades. And these changes are being caused by the "graying" of many societies around the world.[8]

Put simply, demographic graying refers to the fact that many countries around the world (and especially the most developed countries) are becoming, on average, older. As life expectancies have increased dramatically over the past few decades, and as families have had fewer children on average (a consequence of improved material success and standard of living), the "population pyramid," as it is sometimes called, has become inverted. The group at the top of the pyramid—those older and retired citizens—are beginning to outnumber the younger people of working age. And the effect of this graying for governments and their national debts is twofold. First, because people are living longer lives, they are spending more time receiving benefits provided through social welfare programs (programs ubiquitous across developed countries, and even some developing ones), programs predominantly designed when life spans were much shorter. Second, because there are fewer children being born per family, at least in developed societies, the larger group of elderly citizens receiving social welfare benefits must be sustained with tax dollars taken from a shrinking group of younger workers. And unless social welfare benefits are slashed substantially, or tax rates are increased substantially (both difficult political propositions), these changes bode ill for government budgets and budget deficits in the decades ahead.

Again, nothing discussed above is absolutely certain—population growth could come in below estimates due to disease or war or a faster transition to zero population growth, or a huge global economic boom like that after World War II could mitigate the forecasted budget pinch caused by population growth and demographic graying. Further, no two societies will experience an identical confluence of these conditions in the years ahead—some may see population growth sufficient to offset aging populations, but then have to deal with a larger number of citizens with a debt-ridden budget, while others may experience graying but start with a smaller, more manageable debt that offsets the difficulties. Nonetheless, it appears almost certain that at least much of the world is *entering a phase where governments across the globe will need to learn to do more with less.* As populations grow or gray, and in some cases do both, and the ratio of tax-paying workers relative to the number of people receiving social benefits shrinks (or even becomes inverted), governments will likely find themselves spending more on these programs, and on servicing the debt borrowed to pay for these programs, for a larger number of citizens from a shrinking pool of tax dollars contributed by a smaller number of workers.[9]

We need not forecast dramatic and dire events such as a "Global Spring" to illustrate the risks that lie ahead or to highlight the potential trouble governments might find themselves in under these difficult circumstances—although events over the last few years in Spain and Greece, where mostly young, unemployed citizens have taken to the streets to protest austerity measures intended to deal with essentially the same confluence of circumstances involving demography and debt described above, show that something similar is possible even in developed European countries, and not just the developing and turbulent Arab world.[10] Governments are going to have to learn to do more with less, to provide the best, most efficient, and most satisfying possible services to citizens from a shrinking pool of resources. And this is a valuable lesson for governments in times both good and bad, as simply seeking more money to throw at problems has rarely worked well as long-term government policy. So how can governments discover how to do more with less? How can they do so in a way that best meets citizen wants and needs, and perhaps even helps to improve citizen trust, another resource that could grow scarcer in these trying times? Certainly one important solution in these circumstances will be measuring performance in general, in addition to robust citizen satisfaction measurement.

An Interlude: Global Scarcity, Satisfaction Measurement, and Trust

In the material that has been presented in the text up to this point, the practice of citizen satisfaction measurement has been identified as having certain desirable qualities leading to positive ends. Over the last several chapters, for example, we have focused on how citizen satisfaction measurement can help public organizations most efficiently allocate always-limited resources while at the same time improving the services delivered to citizens. By identifying the particular aspects of agencies' or programs' services most conducive to influencing citizen satisfaction, as we exemplified in chapters 4 and 5, governments can focus improvement efforts and resources precisely on those areas most likely to maximize the impact of these efforts, and avoid wasting money elsewhere. As we discussed specifically in chapter 5, satisfaction data can be used as an element within a comprehensive program for improving service delivery and satisfaction across entire national governments, with central institutions working to create a system for government-wide performance improvement. Finally, in several of the preceding chapters we have examined the empirical relationship between satisfying citizens and improving trust in government overall. Not only is citizen satisfaction valuable in its own right, but it also serves as a tool for improving the trust linking state and society, a good that has become limited in supply in nations the world over.

Taken together, the aforementioned benefits of citizen satisfaction measurement all recommend it, we would argue, as one method for addressing at least some of the many challenges facing governments now and in the future. As I have attempted to show above, demographic changes and budget constraints likely mean that governments around the world will be forced to provide better services to a larger number of citizens from a dwindling pool of resources. Failing to do so will likely result in less trusting populations more apt to make the job of governing more difficult still. It may possibly even mean deeply discontented populations like those seen in several nations during the recent Arab Spring. And while no one technique can possibly "solve" all of these issues and provide ready-made answers for how to accomplish these difficult and complicated tasks, citizen satisfaction measurement can help.

More specifically, what governments will need as they enter this challenging era is a broad, deep, and robust international system of citizen satisfaction measurement—a global "International Index of Citizen Satisfaction" (IICS) with measurement conducted within and across nations using a single system and with results available for analysis by researchers and government officials interested in optimizing decision-making processes aimed at improved performance. Not only could such a system help individual governments improve services to their own citizens in a cost-effective manner, but it would also serve as an invaluable source of information for cross-national benchmarking, allowing governments to identify best-in-class performers in offering common services and emulating the practices leading to success. But what would such a cross-national citizen sat-isfaction measurement program look like, and given the complexity and uniqueness of the world's governments, is it even possible? In the next section, we consider some broad but key issues that would need to be addressed to create such an international measurement system.

Towards an International Index of Citizen Satisfaction

In what follows, we outline a series of important issues that require consideration when building the IICS, an idea that has, of late, drawn attention from some prominent international organizations and thought leaders.[11] This list of considerations is certainly not all-encompassing. For example, we will say only a little here about the many, many challenges that would be encountered in conducting this type of massive survey research project, such as the difficul-ties in designing questionnaires and collecting data across dozens of countries with culturally, politically, and economically diverse pop-ulations speaking multiple languages. Nor will we speak in detail about one particular method or model with which this data should be analyzed (though our preferences in this regard should be clear from the preceding chapters). Rather, we intend this exercise to offer a broad outline for such a system of measurement—in academic par-lance, the basis of a "future research agenda"—as well as a list of important, first-order considerations to be taken into account. We also highlight some of the advantages such a system might offer all of the governments measured by and interested in utilizing this type of data to optimize the services delivered to citizens.

- *The IICS should be conducted by (or at minimum, centered in) an international or nongovernmental organization*

It will surprise few readers, I think, to learn that many of the world's governments distrust one another, and are particularly sen-sitive about "being told what to do" by other nation-states or their political leaders. Politicians and the governments they represent tend to protect their national sovereignty jealously, and to resist sugges-tions that other governments may do things better. As such, ideas for improving performance (in any domain, really, including economic and environmental policy, and not just in the arena of government service-delivery performance) are often met with resistance if being advanced by one particular government or another. This is especially so if the government doing the advising is viewed suspiciously, as a hostile foreign power, or has a history of attempting to influence the internal affairs of the country seeking reforms. Given this, the IICS, and really any similar cross-national performance measurement program, will be far more successful if produced independently of any particular state, and instead reside in an international or nongovernmental organization.

An existing project, one produced in a manner similar to how we suggest the IICS should be produced, can be found in the "E-Government Readiness Index," a research project that measures and compares the development of electronic government across nations. This study is produced and published by the United Nations Department of Economic and Social Affairs, and is (much like the proposed IICS) intended to help governments identify national performance leaders (in this case, in delivering e-government services), and thereby in lending guidance to all states hoping to improve their e-government performance. The agenda of the E-Government Readiness Index is undoubtedly advanced by its home within the UN, rather than within any particular UN member state, where claims of bias could more easily be leveled against its findings.

- *The IICS should be inclusive of as many governments around the world as possible*

"'Data! Data! Data!' he cried impatiently. 'I cannot make bricks without clay!'"

—Sherlock Holmes, "The Adventure of the Copper Beeches."

It may be unnecessary to mention, given that we find ourselves entrenched in the age of "Big Data," but more data rather than less is generally helpful in drawing useful conclusions from that data. That is, while "paralysis by analysis" (a phenomenon we discussed in chapter 3) can sometimes overwhelm the researcher confronted with an excess of information, a larger pool of clean, well-crafted and consistent data (more on consistency below) can turn caution or lack of clarity into a decision rendered with greater confidence on both sides. That is, an abundance of data can lend confidence to both the researcher analyzing the data, by bolstering the definitiveness of his or her conclusions, and can also serve to convince skeptical decision-makers that the advice they are receiving is well-founded.

Given this, the IICS ought to undertake measurement of as many governments around the world, and as many departments, agencies, programs, and services within those governments, as possible. A wealth of data that, for instance, measures satisfaction, its drivers, and its outcomes with a most similar type of government agency or service in 100 rather than only three or four countries would certainly lend credibility to findings about performance leaders and laggards, best practices and potential strategies for improvement, and so forth. Benchmarking comparisons based on a dataset this large, and from which researchers find systematically higher satisfaction in those countries that adopted Strategy X in delivering a service rather than Strategy Y, would certainly make a strong case for the former as a best practice that could be replicated elsewhere.

- *Measurement and analysis should focus on cross-national bench-marking for best practice identification*

Connected to these first two ideas, and indeed hinted at in both, is the practice of performance benchmarking towards best practice identification. As we have seen in several of the preceding chapters, citizen satisfaction measurement can be a useful and valuable exercise in its own right—when done by just a single organization within a single nation focused on its own internal practices—for discerning underperforming activities or services, and working to repair them. Yet as we also discussed elsewhere in the book and just a few paragraphs above, one of the most important purposes of satisfaction measurement is to help decision-makers discern how to pursue effective changes for improving services as efficiently as possible, without expensive trial-and-error that could both waste resources and actually harm satisfaction in the long run. And it is here that performance benchmarking becomes most valuable.

We have previously discussed the nature of performance bench-marking in chapters 2 and 4, and given a variety of examples of it in chapter 5, and thus can eschew a lengthy review here. Suffice it to say, while citizen satisfaction measurement of any kind might provide great value to most governments, that value increases expo-nentially if connected to a wide array of comparable measures from similar government programs and services worldwide. This is pre-cisely because the availability of this data could help these govern-ments much more easily identify not only where they are falling short, but what may be working better in other countries, practices not yet implemented in their own context that might help improve satisfaction.

- *Measurement and analysis should focus—at least initially—on ubiquitous government services*

Following on the last two points, the IICS should emphasize mea-surement of one particular subset of government agencies around the world: the most common, ubiquitous programs and services. The 190-plus independent, sovereign nation-states currently occupying the world offer a huge, diverse array of services to citizens. Yet some of these services, and the government agencies tasked with offering them, are decidedly country-specific, focused on an issue or group of citizens endemic to only that country, or perhaps only a few countries in the same region with similar problems to consider. As such, while measurement of these unique kinds of services or agencies could be useful to the specific government offering them, in many cases they may have less to teach other governments about improving their own services. As such, focusing at least initially on the programs, services or agencies offered collectively by a wide array of governments is recommended. Candidates for "most common" government services would certainly include tax collection agencies, public health care and hospitals, social welfare or pension benefits delivery, police and security services, and so forth.

- *The IICS should be grounded in a homogenous, standardized model of citizen satisfaction*

The last three points have discussed how one key benefit of the proposed IICS—and perhaps even the single most important benefit—is the ability to realize improved government performance through benchmarking and the identification of international best practices. Performance benchmarking allows the researcher and/or the data analyst the ability to draw conclusions not only from a particular dataset, but to compare those findings across datasets, and through this to draw conclusions about relative performance and strategies for improving performance. However, as many research practitioners who have attempted to conduct performance benchmarking have quickly realized, this activity can be deeply frustrated by a limited amount or even total absence of truly comparable data. That is, while citizen satisfaction data may exist that could potentially be benchmarked with data from some other study in a different country, noncomparable questionnaires and question wording, modes of data collection, or methods of statistical analysis make comparability problematic, if not impossible.

As such, the proposed IICS should be established around a common model of citizen satisfaction, one using questionnaires as comparable as possible, homogenous item scales, a common method for data analysis (through a single statistical technique), and so forth. In this way, performance benchmarking can be done more accurately, and the conclusions drawn from this process given greater weight.

- *Cultural and national differences must be recognized when conducting measurement and analysis*

To begin this section, we conveniently relieved ourselves of the burden of discussing the many, many difficulties inherent in undertaking a large cross-cultural, multinational research project, the kind of project that involves translating questionnaires into multiple languages and collecting data in many countries simultaneously. Comprehensive works can and have already been written on this subject, and there are far too many issues to discuss here.[12] Yet one consideration involved in this type of research that requires mention is the difficulty inherent in comparing virtually any survey data collected cross-nationally, as this challenge threatens to undermine one of the core purposes of developing an IICS in the first place, the ability to conduct cross-governmental comparisons.

Researchers have long recognized the fact that conducting survey research cross-nationally is fraught with difficulties emanating from cultural difference.[13] Questionnaire translation, scale design, language and dialect idiosyncrasies, and many, many other issues confront the researcher hoping to collect survey data in several countries simultaneously and compare the results accurately and reliably. Most importantly for our purposes vis-à-vis citizen satisfaction measurement, researchers have discovered that respondents from different cultures tend to respond to survey scales differently, meaning that scores (such as the type of 0–100 scaled citizen satisfaction scores presented and discussed in chapters 4, 5, and 6) are oftentimes difficult to compare. If nothing else, this should serve as a warning that more will be entailed in an IICS than cross-national satisfaction measurement and modeling; careful analysis, and possibly even "adjustment" of data based on cultural characteristics, will be needed as well.

- *Measurement and analysis should avoid normative evaluation*

Thus, and as we discussed in the point above, while "culture matters" in this kind of research and must be taken into account, an IICS should avoid entering into normative evaluations of the governments measured to as great an extent as is possible. A large portion of any evaluation of government performance is naturally intertwined with politics, with questions of what government "should do" or "ought to do." Without a doubt, and from its very beginnings, both the study and the practice of politics has been focused on normative issues. Yet to as great an extent as is possible, citizen satisfaction measurement should focus not on alternative *policy* choices or evaluations of the political decisions of particular governments, but rather on the quality of the services provided by the government units tasked with enacting those policies. While such an imperative is undoubtedly difficult to realize—indeed, the author has experienced firsthand in several countries the desire to blame poor service delivery and low citizen satisfaction on the nature of the program or services the political system has sent to the government agency to deliver—the work of an IICS would be significantly undermined if it became tied-up with contestable political positions. Though there is certainly a place for such evaluations, they belong at the national-political level, not within an international system of cross-national citizen satisfaction measurement.

- *Measurement and analysis should focus on linking to objective outcomes, such as financial or budgetary performance, and other "hard" indicators of performance improvement*

While citizen satisfaction research has exploded over the past few decades, both across levels of government and across regions and nations, relatively little research has focused on how citizen satisfaction links-up with demonstrable financial or budgetary outcomes. For example, while research into consumer satisfaction has been found to definitively link to financial outcomes in the private sector for private companies,[14] and to other values like lower complaint rates and stronger customer loyalty, little such research has been conducted for public sector organizations. More specifically, research evidencing the objective, demonstrable benefits to government programs that rigorously measure, monitor and act based on satisfaction data could provide not only general support for this research practice, but also quantitative evidence of its real consequences.

With this imperative in mind, at its inception an IICS should provide not only a citizen satisfaction data repository for use by the world's governments, but also the means for linking satisfaction data to external indicators evidencing the real financial (and other) impacts of satisfaction improvement. For example, evidence showing that some program's satisfaction was improved by X percent through reduced application decision times, and that this improved satisfaction resulted in a gain in an agency's budget through a lessened need for customer service personnel to answer complaints (which dropped X% as well), would clearly illustrate the real financial value of improved satisfaction. And a wealth of this supporting data, collected in numerous countries and available for analysis and comparison, would be better still.

Conclusion

In this chapter, we have reviewed some of the challenges that lie ahead for the world's countries and their governments as they contend with demographic changes and resource constraints. While citizen satisfaction measurement cannot solely and easily solve all of these problems, it can provide one very useful tool for helping governments address them. An IICS, like the one we have broadly outlined above, is thereby recommended, as such a system and the data produced through it could prove extraordinarily helpful for governments seeking cost-effective techniques for both conserving resources and improving citizen satisfaction and citizen trust, doing so in part by learning the best practices of their global neighbors in delivering services.

Appendix

I n what follows, we provide several additional graphs and tables containing statistics overlooked (or more accurately, intentionally omitted) from our discussion of structural equation modeling methods for citizen satisfaction data in chapter 4. While these statistics were omitted because they were deemed too complex and esoteric for the average reader, and probably of less general interest for most reading this book, they are typically reported as a part of the standard output for a Partial Least Squares path model (PLS-PM). These results rely on the same data described and analyzed in chapter 4, and were in fact part of the output produced alongside the data that is now included in figure 4.2. While perhaps of lesser interest to those primarily interested in the practical utilization of satisfaction data and results to improve the performance of and citizen satisfaction with government agencies, these technical details are vital for the serious researcher, whose goal is always a thorough and detail-oriented analysis of the quality of the data, the reliability of the output and estimates, the properties of the overall model that has been estimated, and so forth. But before discussing this output, a few additional words on the method used to estimate the structural equation model provided in chapter 4—PLS-PM—will be useful.

PLS-PM is an iterative structural equation modeling method for simultaneously relating multiple blocks of observed (or manifest) variables to unobserved (or latent) variables (what is called the "measurement modeling" phase), and then relating the resultant latent variables to one another through path coefficients (what is called the "structural modeling" phase). The procedure is an "iterative" one because the specified model is estimated and re-estimated multiple times, and during these iterations the PLS algorithm weights and re-weights the manifest variables within the latent variables until an optimal solution is achieved (called "convergence"). The final model estimation is the one where the weighted latent variables most accurately predict (in terms of explained variance) the endogenous dependent variables. It is through this process that a set of raw survey variables are reduced to a smaller number of latent variables, with each latent variable reflecting a weighted average of its underlying manifests, and "more important" manifests (in terms of their predictive power) receiving greater weight. Finally, these optimally weighted latent variables are then related to one another through ordinary least squares multiple regression (very much like the MLR procedure discussed in chapter 4), producing the path coefficients illustrating the effect of the individual latent variables on the dependent variables.[1]

Because of its computational intensity, PLS-PM can only be implemented using specialized statistical software, and several software packages (such as XLSTAT and SmartPLS) exist for this purpose. For other structural equation modeling techniques—such as covariance-based structural equation modeling (CB-SEM)), which functions similarly to what we have described above but also contains some important differences in both its basic assumptions and in the results produced—different software packages (such as SPSS-AMOS and LISREL) are also available.

Much of the data in table A.1 was previously provided and discussed in chapter 4 (see table 4.2), although the table here includes additional correlations that were not reported. All told, this table includes, first, the mean or average score for each survey question or variable in the sample to be included in our structural equation model—sometimes also called observed or manifest variables in the SEM vernacular—as well as the standard deviation ("SD") for each manifest variable. To the right of these two statistics are bivariate correlations (Pearson's correlations) between each manifest variable, and it is often important to examine these correlations prior to structural equation modeling, at least as an exploratory first step. In the kind of PLS-PM performed here, for instance, we use "reflective" latent variables, which suggest a relationship where the latent variable predicts the manifest variables that underlie it, instead of the other way around. However, this kind of latent variable specification is only appropriate when the underlying manifest variables are highly correlated with one another, and so we would expect any

Table A.1 Descriptive statistics and observed/manifest variable correlations

	MEAN	SD	Overall Exp.	Ease of Info	Clarity of Info	Time. of Process	Ease of Process	Court. of Personnel	Prof. of Personnel	Overall Sat.	Confirm/ Disconfirm	Comp. to Ideal	Complaint	Conf. in Agency	Trust in Govt (Overall)
Overall Exp.	7.12	2.45	1.00	0.45	0.45	0.43	0.44	0.36	0.39	0.52	0.45	0.50	-0.16	0.51	0.27
Ease of Info	7.64	2.49	0.45	1.00	0.73	0.66	0.70	0.55	0.57	0.64	0.60	0.57	-0.24	0.58	0.24
Clarity of Info	7.56	2.46	0.45	0.73	1.00	0.65	0.66	0.58	0.59	0.66	0.61	0.59	-0.24	0.61	0.27
Time. of Process	7.48	2.74	0.43	0.66	0.65	1.00	0.81	0.62	0.63	0.72	0.68	0.64	-0.35	0.65	0.28
Ease of Process	7.44	2.71	0.44	0.70	0.66	0.81	1.00	0.64	0.64	0.75	0.70	0.65	-0.34	0.66	0.28
Court. of Personnel	8.15	2.46	0.36	0.55	0.58	0.62	0.64	1.00	0.87	0.66	0.61	0.57	-0.35	0.61	0.23
Prof. of Personnel	8.21	2.37	0.39	0.57	0.59	0.63	0.64	0.87	1.00	0.69	0.62	0.59	-0.37	0.64	0.24
Overall Sat.	7.54	2.47	0.52	0.64	0.66	0.72	0.75	0.66	0.69	1.00	0.82	0.75	-0.34	0.77	0.31
Confirm/Disconfirm	6.81	2.53	0.45	0.60	0.61	0.68	0.70	0.61	0.62	0.82	1.00	0.74	-0.31	0.73	0.32
Comp. to Ideal	6.52	2.71	0.50	0.57	0.59	0.64	0.65	0.57	0.59	0.75	0.74	1.00	-0.26	0.74	0.34
Complaint	0.11	0.32	-0.16	-0.24	-0.24	-0.35	-0.34	-0.35	-0.37	-0.34	-0.31	-0.26	1.00	-0.29	-0.08
Conf. in Agency	7.09	2.70	0.51	0.58	0.61	0.65	0.66	0.61	0.64	0.77	0.73	0.74	-0.29	1.00	0.38
Trust in Govt (Overall)	4.46	2.54	0.27	0.24	0.27	0.28	0.28	0.23	0.24	0.31	0.32	0.34	-0.08	0.38	1.00

variables we plan to model together within a reflective latent variable to be strongly correlated, and more strongly correlated with one another than with other manifest variables. Beyond this, means, standard deviations, and correlations can provide the researcher with important basic knowledge about the dataset prior to the more complex interpretation of the structural model results, as we previously described in chapter 4.

Figure A.1 provides a technical-graphic presentation of the PLS-PM model we estimated from our citizen satisfaction dataset in chapter 4. The Greek letters displayed—within each latent variable, next to each latent variable, on the paths connecting the variables, and so on—are part of what is called the "LISREL matrix notation system," named for the LISREL statistical software package created for structural equation modeling in the 1970s by the statistician Karl Jorëskog. This matrix notation (which can also be used to display a structural model in row-column algebraic matrix form) and this method of graphically displaying a structural model that the researcher intends to test and estimate is commonly used in the academic literature and more sophisticated research studies. Essentially, a structural model is displayed in this way to provide an abbreviated but complete system for explaining all of the latent variables, manifest variables, manifest-latent relationships, coefficients, error terms, and so on, included within a particular structural equation model.

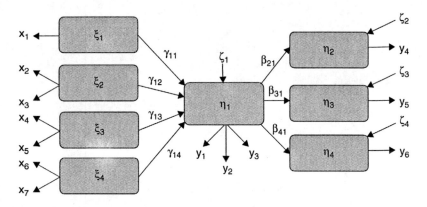

Figure A.1 Graphic PLS-path model with matrix notation.

In general, in this notation system the following Greek characters have these definitions when used to define any structural equation model:[2]

ξ (xi) = Exogenous latent variables

η (eta) = Endogenous latent variables

x = Manifest or observed variables within an exogenous latent variable

y = Manifest or observed variables within an endogenous latent variable

γ (gamma) = Structural coefficients (path estimates) relating exogenous to endogenous variables

β (beta) = Structural coefficients (path estimates) relating endogenous variables to one another

ζ (zeta) = Disturbances or error terms (unexplained variance) for endogenous variables

In the model in figure A.1, therefore, the specific notations refer to the following exogenous and endogenous variables:[3]

ξ_1 = Expectations

ξ_2 = Information

ξ_3 = Process

ξ_4 = Customer Service

η_1 = Citizen Satisfaction

η_2 = Complaint Rate

η_3 = Confidence

η_4 = Overall Trust

Furthermore, the manifest variables included in the model are defined as:

x_1 = Overall expectations

x_2 = Ease of accessing information (in Information)

x_3 = Clarity of information (in Information)

x_4 = Timeliness of the process (in Process)

x_5 = Ease of the process (in Process)

x_6 = Courtesy of customer service personnel (in Customer Service)

x_7 = Professionalism of customer service personnel (in Customer Service)

y_1 = Overall satisfaction (in Citizen Satisfaction)
y_2 = Confirmation/disconfirmation of expectations (in Citizen Satisfaction)
y_3 = Comparison to an ideal (in Citizen Satisfaction)
y_4 = Complaint rate
y_5 = Confidence in the agency
y_6 = Overall trust in Washington, D.C.

Finally, the ζ connected to each endogenous latent variable (ζ_1 through ζ_4) represents the error term (or unexplained variance) for that respective latent variable.

Table A.2 provides the most important results for what is known as the "outer" or measurement model of a structural equation model, and these results show the correlation between each manifest variable and both its own latent variable and all of the other latent variables included in the model. Also called "standard loadings" or "factor loadings," the relationship between each manifest variable and its latent variable is determined through the iterative weighting and re-weighting process described earlier. In PLS-PM, this table of output is examined first and foremost as an initial check for both convergent and discriminant validity. Convergent validity exists if

Table A.2 Model loadings and cross-loadings

	LV Expect	LV Info	LV Process	LV CSR	LV Cit. Sat.	LV Comp	LV Confidence	LV Trust
Overall Exp.	1.000	0.515	0.491	0.403	0.540	−0.205	0.520	0.268
Ease of Info	0.487	0.934	0.747	0.600	0.687	−0.313	0.652	0.269
Clarity of Info	0.479	0.941	0.736	0.634	0.721	−0.348	0.691	0.293
Time. of Process	0.473	0.755	0.961	0.656	0.803	−0.407	0.740	0.325
Ease of Process	0.471	0.764	0.960	0.675	0.796	−0.395	0.739	0.295
Court. of Personnel	0.375	0.633	0.675	0.968	0.678	−0.360	0.633	0.226
Prof. of Personnel	0.407	0.643	0.668	0.970	0.700	−0.382	0.650	0.236
Overall Sat.	0.521	0.718	0.796	0.704	0.940	−0.427	0.806	0.318
Confirm/Disconfirm	0.479	0.699	0.786	0.658	0.942	−0.388	0.784	0.349
Comp. to Ideal	0.507	0.678	0.739	0.619	0.907	−0.346	0.778	0.345
Complaint	−0.205	−0.353	−0.418	−0.383	−0.417	1.000	−0.385	−0.107
Conf. in Agency	0.520	0.717	0.770	0.662	0.849	−0.385	1.000	0.377
Trust in Govt (Overall)	0.268	0.300	0.323	0.239	0.362	−0.107	0.377	1.000

the manifest variables included in a single latent variable are sufficiently strongly correlated with one another and the latent variable they "occupy," which suggests that they are indeed a part of the same conceptual phenomenon. On the other hand, discriminant validity exists if the manifest variables are sufficiently unrelated to the other latent variables to be included in the model, that is, if the researcher isn't just treating a large number of variables as distinct phenomena that actually tap into the same one phenomenon in slightly different ways. In this portion of the analysis, then, the key check is to see that each manifest variable is strongly correlated with its own latent variable, and more strongly correlated than it is with any other latent variable.

Table A.3 provides goodness-of-fit measures (sometimes also called reliability or convergent validity measures) for each latent variable included in our structural equation model. The two most commonly used measures of latent variable goodness-of-fit for a PLS-PM model are Cronbach's α and average variance extracted (AVE), and each uses a slightly different approach for computing the strength of the inter-item relationships among the manifest variables included in a latent variable. (Because Expectations, Complaints, Confidence and Trust are not, in point of fact, latent variables—as each includes only a single manifest variable, making them observed variables in this structural model—no goodness-of-fit measures are provided for these variables.) In general, AVE values > 0.50 and α values > 0.75 are considered sufficient to deem a latent variable valid

Table A.3   Latent variable goodness-of-fit

	Cronbach's α	AVE
Expect	NA	NA
Info	0.86	0.88
Process	0.92	0.92
CSR	0.94	0.94
ACSI	0.92	0.86
Comp	NA	NA
Confidence	NA	NA
Trust	NA	NA

and reliable. In this instance, all of our latent variables easily exceed these thresholds, suggesting that our latent variables are indeed well constructed.

Table A.4 provides bivariate correlations (again, Pearson's correlations) between all of the estimated latent variables included in our structural equation model. These correlations are produced once scores for the latent variables have been created as weighted averages of their manifest variables through the iterative algorithmic process described earlier. In the first instance, these correlations are often examined as an additional test of discriminant validity, much as we did with the data in table A.2. In this case, we would examine the correlations between each latent variable to confirm that none are too strongly correlated with one another, which again could indicate that we are measuring the same concept in multiple, only slightly different ways. While there are no hard and fast rules about what level of correlation violates discriminant validity, in this example the strong correlation between Citizen Satisfaction and Confidence may (at least superficially) give us cause to reexamine our survey instrument and make certain the questions asked there were sufficiently different. However, given the level of data aggregation in the dataset we are working with (thousands of cases across multiple years, and dozens of different government programs and agencies), as well as the prior theoretical expectation that satisfaction would be a very strong predictor of confidence, the strong correlation here would most likely not cause us to alter our model. Finally, latent variable

Table A.4 Latent variable correlations

	LV Expect	LV Info	LV Process	LV CSR	LV ACSI	LV Comp	LV Confidence	LV Trust
Expect	1.000	0.515	0.491	0.403	0.540	−0.205	0.520	0.268
Info	0.515	1.000	0.791	0.658	0.751	−0.353	0.717	0.300
Process	0.491	0.791	1.000	0.693	0.832	−0.418	0.770	0.323
CSR	0.403	0.658	0.693	1.000	0.711	−0.383	0.662	0.239
ACSI	0.540	0.751	0.832	0.711	1.000	−0.417	0.849	0.362
Comp	−0.205	−0.353	−0.418	−0.383	−0.417	1.000	−0.385	−0.107
Confidence	0.520	0.717	0.770	0.662	0.849	−0.385	1.000	0.377
Trust	0.268	0.300	0.323	0.239	0.362	−0.107	0.377	1.000

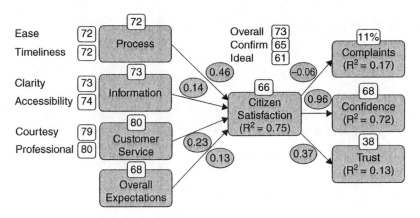

Figure A.2 Complete graphic model results.

Note: All coefficients/path estimates significant at P<0.001.

correlations can often be interesting in their own right, as they can give the researcher a more expansive look at which variables are most strongly correlated, regardless of the specific paths/coefficients we have estimated in our structural model.

Figure A.2 provides the final, completed structural equation model, which displays the path estimates (the unstandardized regression coefficients) connecting each independent to each dependent latent variable, the mean score for each latent variable (again transformed to a 0–100 scale using the methods described in chapter 4), and the R^2 (or total variance explained) for each endogenous latent variable in the model. Because these results were first provided and more thoroughly discussed in chapter 4, this output and its interpretation needs no further explanation.

The data included in table A.5 provides an additional means for determining the relative importance of the exogenous latent variables in predicting our key endogenous variable, Citizen Satisfaction. In particular, the data in the last two rows is often used to make these importance determinations (the first two rows repeat the correlations and path coefficients already provided, and then multiply these two statistics). The data here shows the relative contribution of each latent variable to the total prediction of Citizen Satisfaction ("Contribution to R^2," as a percentage), and the "Cumulative R^2"

Table A.5 Contribution of the variables to the prediction of citizen satisfaction

	LV Process	LV Info	LV CSR	LV Expect
Correlation	0.832	0.751	0.711	0.540
Path Coefficient	0.510	0.141	0.212	0.132
Correlation * Path Coefficient	0.424	0.106	0.151	0.071
Contribution to R^2	56.4%	14.0%	20.0%	9.5%
Cumulative R^2	56.4%	70.5%	90.5%	100.0%

Table A.6 Model goodness-of-fit measures

	GoF	GoF (Boot.)	SE	CR	Upper (95%)	Lower (95%)
Relative	0.986	0.982	0.016	63.478	0.939	1.000

shows increases to total R^2 as we "add" the predictive effect of each latent variable in a step-wise fashion. What these results illustrate is that, as we concluded in chapter 4, Process is clearly the most important variable in terms of predicting Citizen Satisfaction, as this variable alone is responsible for explaining more than 56 percent of the variance in Citizen Satisfaction.

Finally, Table A.6 provides one common goodness-of-fit measure for determining the overall quality of a PLS path model. In PLS-PM, which focuses on the explained variance of the endogenous latent variables rather than, for instance, the global fit of a covariance matrix (like maximum likelihood estimation covariance-based structural equation modeling techniques), the "GoF" estimate is produced using the geometric mean of the average communality index and the average R^2 value of the endogenous latent variables.[4] Again, while no hard and fast rules exist for deeming a relative GoF value acceptable, a model with a relative GoF greater than 0.90 is usually considered a "good model."

Notes

Introduction

1. Throughout the text, I will freely and interchangeably use the terms "citizen," "customer," "consumer," and "user"—and at times compounds of two of these nouns, such as "citizen-user" or "citizen-customer"—to reference those individuals to be interviewed about their satisfaction with a government service, or with the government agency delivering that service. While some might resist the notion of referring to individuals experiencing government services as "customers" or "citizens"—the former because the term implies that government is or ought to function like a private sector company, the latter because it implies that only a certain class of residents of a nation ought to receive government services—these terms are used only for the sake of ease and convenience, and should not be viewed to endorse one view on the relationship between the individual and the state over another.

2. This line appears in Act IV, Scene I of the play.

3. Shortly after writing on this book began, a team of archaeologists from Texas State University announced that they had discovered what they believed to be the flagship of legendary pirate Henry Morgan (today known mainly for the spiced rum that bears his name) off the coast of Panama. Lost in 1671, the ship had been captured from France and renamed by Morgan "Satisfaction." While the exact meaning of the name for Morgan is unclear, it seems more likely to have been a reference to pleasure, fulfillment, happiness, or contentment than to "atonement for sin," given Morgan's infamous line of work.

4. For some examples, see: R. Hoppock and C. L. Odom. 1940. "Job Satisfaction." *Occupations: The Vocational Guidance Journal* 19(1): 24–29; G. B. Hotchkiss. 1925. "An Economic Defence of Advertising." *The American Economic Review* 15(1): 14–22; B. W. Lewis. 1938. "The 'Consumer' and 'Public' Interests under Public Regulation." *The Journal of Political Economy* 46(1): 97–107; C. F. Phillips. 1941.

"A Critical Analysis of Recent Literature Dealing with Marketing Efficiency." *The Journal of Marketing* 5(4): 360–365; A. J. Spector. 1956. "Expectations, Fulfillment, and Morale." *The Journal of Abnormal and Social Psychology* 52(1): 51–56; D. E. Super. 1939. "Occupational Level and Job Satisfaction." *Journal of Applied Psychology* 23(5): 547–564; E. K. Strong. 1925. "Theories of Selling." *Journal of Applied Psychology* 9(1): 75–86.

5. For Simon's most prominent works on the topic, see: H. A. Simon. 1947. *Administrative Behavior.* New York: Free Press; H. A. Simon. 1952. "A Comparison of Organisation Theories." *The Review of Economic Studies* 20(1): 40–48.

6. There is a wealth of literature on citizen satisfaction with police services and urban government between 1965 and 1990. Some of this includes early writings by Elinor Ostrom, who would go on to receive the Nobel Prize in Economics in 2009. For some examples, see: E. Ostrom, R. B. Parks, and G. P. Whitaker. 1973. "Do We Really Want To Consolidate Urban Police Forces? A Reappraisal of Some Old Assertions." *Public Administration Review* 33(5): 423–432; E. Ostrom et al. 1979. "Evaluating Police Organization." *Public Productivity Review* 3(3): 3–27. See also: B. Stipak. 1979. "Citizen Satisfaction with Urban Services: Potential Misuse as a Performance Indicator." *Public Administration Review* 39(1): 46–52; R. Stagner. 1970. "Perceptions, Aspirations, Frustrations, and Satisfactions: An Approach to Urban Indicators." *The ANNALS of the American Academy of Political and Social Science* 388(1): 59–68.

7. To illustrate the importance of local government citizen satisfaction research, the International City/County Management Association (ICMA), the most prominent international association for local government practitioners, is deeply involved in developing and deploying citizen satisfaction survey questions that can be easily applied by local government officials (i.e., mayors, city managers, etc.) in their own jurisdictions.

8. For some examples, see: C. J. Anderson and C.A. Guillory. 1997. "Political Institutions and Satisfaction with Democracy: A Cross-National Analysis of Consensus and Majoritarian Systems." *American Political Science Review* 91(1): 66–81; T. R. Cusack. 1999. "The Shaping of Popular Satisfaction with Government and Regime Performance in Germany." *British Journal of Political Science* 29: 641–672; G. Serra. 1995. "Citizen-Initiated Contact and Satisfaction with Bureaucracy: A Multivariate Analysis." *Journal of Public Administration Research and Theory* 5(2): 175–188; G. G. Van Ryzin and E. W. Freeman. 1997.

"Viewing Organizations as Customers of Government Services: Data from Maryland's Housing Development Programs." *Public Productivity & Management Review* 20(4): 419–431.

9. For more background on the NPM movement, see: L. Kaboolian. 1998. "The New Public Management: Challenging the Boundaries of the Administration vs. Management Debate." *Public Administration Review* 58(3): 189–93.

10. Noted satisfaction researcher Richard Oliver has defined satisfaction (2010) as: "the consumer's fulfillment response. It is a judgment that a product/service feature, or the product or service itself, provided (or is providing) a *pleasurable* level of consumption-related fulfillment, including levels of under- or overfulfillment."

11. As part of its original and enduring research mission, much of the ACSI data (for both the public and private sectors) is publicly available on the ACSI website. Readers interested in accessing this data can visit the website at: www.theacsi.org.

1 Government Performance Measurement Comes of Age

1. For this quote, see: H. P. Hatry. 2006. *Performance Measurement: Getting Results* (Washington, DC: Urban Institute Press), p. 2.

2. While we will not discuss it at length in what follows, another watershed moment in the evolution of government performance measurement, at least in the United States at the federal level, predates all of the initiatives we will focus on here: the creation of the OMB in 1970. OMB's core mission of assisting the president in both creating the budget and overseeing the quality and efficiency of federal government programs and services remains a central feature in the performance measurement universe at this level of government today.

3. The Civil Service Reform Act of 1883 (also known as the Pendleton Act) provides one much earlier example of federal government reform aimed at government performance improvement (by placing merit above politics in the hiring of federal employees), but it had little to do with performance measurement per se.

4. Most scholars attribute the increased interest in government performance measurement to the loosely related "Reinventing Government" and "New Public Management" movements begun in the 1990s, popular both within the United States and abroad. For further information on these movements, see: L. R. Jones. and F. Thompson. 1999. *Public Management: Institutional Renewal for the Twenty-First Century* (Stamford, CT: JAI Press); D. F. Kettl. 2000. *The Global Public*

Management Revolution: A Report on the Transformation of Governance (Washington, DC: Brookings Institution Press).

5. For a review of these types of performance measures as they apply to government services, see: J. Kelly and D. Swindell. 2002. "A Multiple Indicator Approach to Municipal Service Evaluation: Correlating Performance and Citizen Satisfaction across Jurisdictions." *Public Administration Review* 62(5): 610–621.

6. For a fuller discussion of PBB, see: J. Melkers and K. Willoughby. 1998. "The State of the States: Performance-Based Budgeting Requirements in 47 out of 50." *Public Administration Review* 58(1): 66–73.

7. In chapter 3, we will review a substantial selection of these kinds of variables, which are often included in a satisfaction questionnaire and a satisfaction statistical model as determinants (or influencing factors) vis-à-vis citizen satisfaction.

8. It is important to mention here that in no way should internal and external measures of performance be thought of as at odds or mutually exclusive. Indeed, the two often go hand-in-hand and are sometimes implemented in tandem, and in creative ways that connect one to another. Nevertheless, the simple dichotomy we provide here is useful in understanding the arguments we make later.

9. For a relatively early statement on this phenomenon, see: G. D. Wagenheim and J. H. Reurink 1991. "Customer Service in Public Administration." *Public Administration Review* 51(3): 263–270.

10. For more information on this shift from supplier to consumer-oriented power in the Information Age, see: C. Fornell. 2007. *The Satisfied Customer: Winners and Losers in the Battle for Buyer Preference* (New York: Palgrave Macmillan); B. Rezabakhshet al. 2006. "Consumer Power: A Comparison of the Old Economy and the Internet Economy." *Journal of Consumer Policy* 29(1): 3–36.

11. For a review of the IT revolution and its immense importance in the private sector, see: S. Mithas, S. 2011. *Digital Intelligence: What Every Smart Manager Must Have for Success in an Information Age* (North Potomac, MD: Finerplanet).

12. Ford once famously wrote, "any customer can have a car painted any color that he wants so long as it is black," pretty clearly indicating his opposition to consumer power.

13. For a review of this development, see: Fornell, *The Satisfied Customer.*

14. A cursory review of the academic marketing literature over the past two decades will clearly evidence the increased prevalence of these terms, and the focus on these practices. Moreover, it is now common for corporate executives to tout his or her company's performance on these kind of

metrics, often including them as part of a "dashboard" of "key performance indicators" (KPI).

15. For a review of the importance of the private sector in setting public sector management and measurement reform agenda over the past few decades, see B. G. Peters. 2001. *The Politics of Bureaucracy* (London, UK: Routledge).

16. In chapter 7, we will discuss the interconnections between the Information Age, increased democratic sovereignty, and the need for citizen satisfaction measurement in greater detail, and from an interesting perspective (we think).

2 The Purposes and Objectives of Citizen Satisfaction Measurement

1. For a very good study that investigates the relationship between customer satisfaction with private sector firms and a variety of financial measures, see: N. A. Morgan and L. L. Rego. 2006. "The Value of Different Customer Satisfaction and Loyalty Metrics in Predicting Business Performance." *Marketing Science* 25(5): 426–439.

2. The preceding example assumes we are focused on a central or national government, the type of government where "defection" means leaving one's native land for another. It is somewhat easier for citizens to defect from one local government to another (i.e., to move from one county, city, town, or municipality, or even state or province, to another) in much the same way consumers switch companies. It is not at all uncommon to hear of citizens moving in large numbers from one city to a neighboring city to get better police protection, better fire protection, a better natural environment, new neighbors, closer proximity to shopping and entertainment, and so on, and in this way local government operates somewhat more like a free market. (The American experience with "white flight" from urban centers beginning in the 1950s is one historically significant example of this type of defection from local government.) But even this type of defection from government carries higher direct and indirect costs (e.g., moving expenses, making children switch schools and leave friends behind, etc.), much higher than a vast majority of private sector goods and services.

3. While the data shown in the graph reflects results from just a single calendar year of measurement (2011), these results have been consistent for more than a decade.

4. For a discussion of the "positives" of complaining customers in the private sector, see: C. Fornell. 2007. *The Satisfied Customer: Winners and Losers in the Battle for Buyer Preference* (New York: Palgrave Macmillan).

5. For a review of these laws, see: J. M. Ackerman and I. E. Sandoval-Ballesteros. 2006. "The Global Explosion of Freedom of Information Laws." *Administrative Law Review* 58(1): 85–130.
6. In March of 2011, Eric K. Shinseki, secretary of Veterans Affairs, used ACSI data and results to evidence the strong performance of the US National Cemetery Administration (NCA) in testimony before the US Congress. The full text of his comments can be found at: www.va.gov/OCA/testimony/svac/SecVABudgetTestimony2012SVAC.asp. Furthermore, the federal government's "Program Assessment Rating Tool," enacted under George W. Bush, and the "Government Performance and Results Act of 1993" (GPRA) both mandate that most federal agencies annually provide OMB with ratings on customer satisfaction surveys of some kind for the same purpose.
7. For this quote, see: M. Warren. 1999. "Introduction," in Mark Warren (ed.), *Democracy and Trust,* UK: Cambridge University Press, p. 2.
8. In chapter 6, we provide a much fuller, more detailed account of how and why trust has declined.
9. For a discussion of the decline in trust in democratic governments, see: S. J. Pharr and R. D. Putnam (Eds.). 2000. *Disaffected Democracies: What's Troubling the Trilateral Countries?* (Princeton, NJ: Princeton University Press); R. D. Putnam. 2000. *Bowling Alone: The Collapse and Revival of American Community* (New York: Simon & Schuster).
10. For a review of the history of performance benchmarking in the private sector, see: R. J. Boxwell. 1994. *Benchmarking for Competitive Advantage* (New York: McGraw Hill).
11. A. Kouzmin et al. 1999. "Benchmarking and Performance Measurement in Public Sectors." *International Journal of Public Sector Management* 12(2): 121–144. For a thorough review of government benchmarking, see: P. S. Keehley et al. 1997. *Benchmarking for Best Practices in the Public Sector: Achieving Performance Breakthroughs in Federal, State, and Local Agencies* (San Francisco, CA: Jossey-Bass).
12. "Program Assessment Rating Tool Guidance No. 2007–02," Office of Management and Budget, p. 74, available at: www.whitehouse.gov/sites/default/files/omb/part/fy2007/2007_guidance_final.pdf.

3 The Practice of Citizen Satisfaction Measurement: Unit of Analysis Selection, Questionnaire Design, and Data Collection

1. For an example of early research in this area, see: E. Ostrom, R. B. Parks, and G. P. Whitaker. 1973. "Do We Really Want to Consolidate Urban Police Forces? A Reappraisal of Some Old Assertions." *Public

Administration Review 33(5): 423–432. Also see: B. Stipak. 1979. "Citizen Satisfaction with Urban Services: Potential Misuse as a Performance Indicator." *Public Administration Review* 39(1): 46–52.

2. T. H. Poister and J. C. Thomas. 2011. "The Effect of Expectations and Expectancy Confirmation/Disconfirmation on Motorists' Satisfaction with State Highways." *Journal of Public Administration Research and Theory* 21(4): 601–617.

3. For a recent example of research in this area, see: F. V. Morgeson III and C. Petrescu. 2011. "Do They All Perform Alike? An Examination of Perceived Performance, Citizen Satisfaction and Trust with U.S. Federal Agencies." *International Review of Administrative Sciences* 77(3): 451–479.

4. For a good reference on the phenomenon that is "political marketing," see: N. J. O'Shaughnessy and S. C. Henneberg (Eds.). 2002. *The Idea of Political Marketing* (Westport, CT: Greenwood Publishing Group).

5. For instance, the Gallup Poll is just one example of a daily tracking study of presidential approval, and virtually every major news outlet now conducts its own approval polls for both the president and Congress.

6. The term "democratic deficit" is often used in relation to (and may have been coined in regards to) the European Union, which has grown decidedly more powerful over the last few decades, but which exercises most of its power through insulated bureaucratic institutions instead of elective democratic institutions.

7. One technique used by administrative institutions in many democracies to enhance communication between them and the citizens they serve is the "public comment" process, yet most still argue that administrative institutions and their processes remain too far removed from the ordinary citizen. For a classic statement on the problems of growing administrative authority, particularly in the American context, see: T. J. Lowi. 1969. *The End of Liberalism: The Second Republic of the United States* (New York: W.W. Norton). For recent advances in the public comment process, see: Morgeson III, F. V. 2005. *Reconciling Democracy and Bureaucracy: Towards a Deliberative-Democratic Model of Bureaucratic Accountability* (PhD diss., University of Pittsburgh).

8. In survey research, a "population" is typically defined as a discrete group of individuals that possesses at least one common characteristic, the group that the survey researcher wants to collect data from. In this case, the one "common characteristic" to be focused on is experience with one or several administrative institutions, the kind of experience that will allow the citizen to adequately report on their experiences and

gauge their satisfaction. On the other hand, a "sample" of a population is most often defined as a representative cross-section less than the whole of the entire population that shares the common characteristic. We further clarify the definitions of these two entities in regards to satisfaction measurement of bureaucracies below.

9. This matter relates somewhat to the issue of questionnaire design discussed later, and specifically to the inclusion of "screening" questions in a survey, but most satisfaction studies, when collecting data, screen potential respondents for recent actual experience before proceeding to interviewing on the full questionnaire. For instance, for a local government police services questionnaire, potential respondents might be asked: "Have you had any direct contact with your local police in the past year?" For the federal government, a screening question might read: "Have you had direct experience and contact with any U.S. federal government agencies in the past year?" Only a respondent who answers "yes" to one of these screening questions would then be asked the full slate of survey questions.

10. If the nature or purpose of these "drivers" and "outcomes" of satisfaction are still unclear, the statistical modeling techniques used in the next chapter should further clarify them, and chapter 5 will illustrate precisely how this data can be applied for practical, process improvement purposes.

11. For a more complete discussion of the topic, found especially in the book's first chapter, see: R. L. Oliver. 2010. *Satisfaction: A Behavioral Perspective on the Consumer* (New York: ME Sharpe Incorporated). For a very good, although now slightly "old," review of competing perspectives on how to measure satisfaction, see: Y. Yi. 1990. "A Critical Review of Consumer Satisfaction." *Review of Marketing* 4(1): 68–123.

12. In psychometric terms, satisfaction is what is called an "unobservable phenomenon," meaning something that cannot be directly observed and measured by the researcher, because existing only "inside the head" of the individual as an attitude, belief, opinion, and so on. Nevertheless, attempts to measure satisfaction directly through proxies have been attempted, but mostly unsuccessfully.

13. In addition to the Yi (1990) article cited above, for evidence of the superiority of cumulative measures of satisfaction in predicting outcome measures, see: L. L. Olsen and M. D. Johnson. 2003. "Service Equity, Satisfaction, and Loyalty: From Transaction-Specific to Cumulative Evaluations." *Journal of Service Research* 5(3): 184–195.

14. While we cannot know for sure, it is most likely the case that organizations that advertise a "97% satisfaction rate" use what is known as a "top-box" measure of satisfaction. On this technique, the researcher will (very

arbitrarily) take the top few numbers on a scale, deem them as indicative of "satisfied" respondents, and then report the percentage of those respondents from the whole sample as satisfied. So for example, if satisfaction is measured on a 10-point scale, the researcher using top-box might decide that anyone who answers 7, 8, 9, or 10 is "satisfied," and so if 97 percent of the sample answers in that range, satisfaction is reported at 97 percent. The major problem with this approach is the unscientific—and often self-serving—determination of which responses on the scale should count as satisfied, and the way the resulting statistic often badly misrepresents the underlying distribution of the responses.

15. For a comprehensive reference book that addresses these and many other issues, see: P. V. Marsden and J. D. Wright (Eds.). 2010. *Handbook of Survey Research*, 2nd ed. (UK: Emerald Group Publishing). For another excellent work on the subject, see: A. N. Oppenheim. 1992. *Questionnaire Design, Interviewing and Attitude Measurement*, 3rd ed. (New York: Continuum Publishing).

16. To offer a rough guideline for questionnaire length, most ACSI questionnaires—like those used to collect much of the data we analyze in the remaining chapters—contain between 20 and 35 questions only, including the questions for variables influencing satisfaction, the satisfaction questions, and the outcome questions, along with demographic questions, and screening and segmentation questions.

17. For a more detailed look at these and other questions as asked in the ACSI study specifically, including full question wording, scales, demographic questions, and so on, see: Morgeson III and Petrescu. 2011. "Do They All Perform Alike?" 451–479; F. V. Morgeson III, D. VanAmburg, and S. Mithas. 2011. "Misplaced Trust? Exploring the Structure of the E-Government-Citizen Trust Relationship." *Journal of Public Administration Research and Theory* 21(2): 257–83; F. V. Morgeson III and S. Mithas. 2009. "Does E-Government measure up to E-Business? Comparing End-user Perceptions of U.S. Federal Government and E-Business Websites." *Public Administration Review* 69(4): 740–52; F. V. Morgeson III. 2011. "Comparing Determinants of Website Satisfaction and Loyalty across the E-Government and E-Business Domains." *Electronic Government: An International Journal* 8(2/3): 164–84; F. V. Morgeson III. 2013. "Expectations, Disconfirmation, and Citizen Satisfaction with the US Federal Government: Testing and Expanding the Model." *Journal of Public Administration Research and Theory* 23(2): 289–305.

18. For an introductory volume on survey sampling, see: R. L. Scheaffer et al. 2012. *Elementary Survey Sampling*, 3rd ed. (Boston, MA: Cengage Learning).

19. For a review of the incident in the history of survey sampling that still serves as the most common example of good versus poor methods, and the consequences it had for drawing (incorrect) inferences, the "Literary Digest" affair of 1936, see: P. Squire. 1988. "Why the 1936 Literary Digest Poll Failed." *Public Opinion Quarterly* 52 (1): 125–133.

4 The Practice of Citizen Satisfaction Measurement: Statistical Analysis and Modeling

1. Data for each of these annual studies was collected during the months of July, August, and September in each of these years, and sought interview respondents who had experienced a federal government service at any time over the prior 12 months. Moreover, each of these annual samples was collected using two data collection methods in roughly equal proportions, the two methods outlined in chapter 3: Random digit-dial, computer-assisted telephone interviewing, and online, Internet panel interviewing.

2. The smaller "N" for some of the variables, less than the maximum "N" of 7204 for the overall satisfaction question, provides an example of the "missing data" problem that is experienced in almost any study of this kind. Missing data occurs because, for a variety of reasons, respondents are either unable or unwilling to answer certain questions in a survey. For instance, the relatively large number of missing cases for the "courtesy" and "professionalism" questions is due to the fact that most respondents have not contacted a government agency and interacted with a customer service representative. For a discussion of various methods of how to treat missing data during analysis, see: C. K. Enders. 2010. *Applied Missing Data Analysis* (New York: The Guilford Press).

3. For more information on *t*-tests and a wide assortment of other tests of statistical significance, which tell the researcher that the difference between two variable means is "real," see: D. J. Sheskin. 2004. *Handbook of Parametric and Nonparametric Statistical Procedures*, 3rd ed. (Boca Raton, FL: CRC Press).

4. Careful review of these numbers will show that each variable has a correlation of exactly "1" with itself, meaning a perfect correlation, which is correct and to be expected; any variable always perfectly covaries with itself, obviously.

5. It is important to note, and I have tried to avoid in how I have worded the matter here, one of the most basic rules of statistical analysis: *Correlation does not necessarily imply causation.* While correlation analysis can tell us how two variables tend to move together within

a sample, it cannot tell us that the movement in one variable "causes" the movement in another. It is the job of theory, and sometimes an understanding of actual practices and good common sense, to help us determine which factors we think "precede" and thereby may "cause" others.

6. For a solid yet short and reasonably simple introduction to multiple regression techniques, see: P. D. Allison. 1999. *Multiple Regression: A Primer* (Thousand Oaks, CA: Pine Forge Press). For another very good volume on the topic, also see: W. D. Berry. 1993. *Understanding Regression Assumptions* (Newbury Park, CA: Sage Publications).

7. Researchers will sometimes examine the "Standardized Estimates" when comparing regression coefficients in an MLR model, as these coefficients correct for differences in coefficient size based solely on differences in standard deviations, differences produced by either greater variance in a variable, or the scale on which the survey question was asked. However, since all of our variables have the same scale and very similar standard deviations, the standardized and unstandardized estimates are quite similar as well, and our conclusions in this example would be largely unchanged if we focused on either.

8. Another, more complex issue within MLR analyses is the existence of strong correlations between two or more of the independent or predictor variables, a problem known as "multicollinearity." When multicollinearity is present in data—and indeed, multicollinearity exists in the dataset we are analyzing here, as confirmed by "variance inflation factor" (VIF) tests (not shown), and afflicts this data because of the strong correlations between some of the similar predictor variables ("courtesy" and "professionalism" of personnel, for instance)—both coefficients and tests of significant can become less reliable, along with the reliability of the results themselves. While we won't go into great detail on the subject, the SEM procedures discussed below are more trustworthy under conditions of multicollinearity, precisely because they take strongly correlated variables and model them together in latent variables that assume these strong relationships.

9. Sewall Wright is typically credited with being the "father of structural equation modeling." See: S. Wright. 1921. "Correlation and Causation." *Journal of Agricultural Research* XX(7): 557–587. For a very good and more recent overview of SEM techniques, see: R. O. Mueller. 1995. *Basic Principles of Structural Equation Modeling: An Introduction to LISREL and EQS* (New York: Springer).

10. For a few more recent works that employ SEM methods to model and analyze citizen satisfaction data, see: F. V. Morgeson III. 2011.

"Comparing Determinants of Website Satisfaction and Loyalty across the E-Government and E-Business Domains." *Electronic Government: An International Journal* 8(2/3): 164–84; F. V. Morgeson III and C. Petrescu. 2011. "Do They All Perform Alike? An Examination of Perceived Performance, Citizen Satisfaction and Trust with U.S. Federal Agencies." *International Review of Administrative Sciences* 77(3): 451–479; H. Park and J. Blenkinsopp. 2011. "The Roles of Transparency and Trust in the Relationship between Corruption and Citizen Satisfaction." *International Review of Administrative Sciences* 77(2): 254–274; C, G. Reddick and J. Roy. 2012. "Business Perceptions and Satisfaction with E-government: Findings from a Canadian Survey," *Government Information Quarterly* 30(1): 1–9; G. G. Van Ryzin et al. 2004. "Drivers and Consequences of Citizen Satisfaction: An Application of the American Customer Satisfaction Index Model to New York City." *Public Administration Review* 64(3): 331–41.

11. While there is some disagreement on this topic, many researchers agree that multiple-item latent variables provide more robust, more precise measures (i.e., measures less prone to error) than single-item measures, precisely because they minimize measurement error by "triangulating" a phenomenon with multiple, interrelated survey questions. Where there is no disagreement is in the usefulness of latent variables to "reduce dimensions" in data, allowing the inclusion of a larger number of highly correlated variables in a single model, something that is often impossible in MLR.

12. This type of model of citizen satisfaction data, sometimes termed a "performance-satisfaction-trust" model, has been increasingly used by a range of academic researchers and practitioners. For a more in-depth review of the theoretical foundations and statistical tools used in this kind of modeling, see: G. Bouckaert and S. Van de Walle. 2003. "Comparing Measures of Citizen Trust and User Satisfaction as Indicators of "Good Governance." *International Review of Administrative Sciences* 69(3): 329–343; Morgeson III and Petrescu. "Do They All Perform Alike?" 451–479; G. G. Van Ryzin. 2007. "Pieces of a Puzzle: Linking Government Performance, Citizen Satisfaction and Trust." *Public Performance & Management Review* 30(4): 521–535.

13. The simple formula used here to make the transformation from a 1–10 to a 0–100 scale is: $(\bar{x}-1)/9\times100$. In the case of the latent variable mean scores, this transformation for each survey item included in the latent would be undertaken, and then the mean score for each manifest variable would be multiplied by its normalized weight, with the sum of these reflecting the transformed, weighted mean score for the latent variable.

14. ACSI, the project for which this data was originally collected, uses Partial Least Squares path modeling (PLS-PM), a specific type of structural equation modeling to weight the individual questions (or manifest variables) into the latent variables (the "measurement model"), and to create the coefficients linking the latent variables (the "structural model"). Put simply, the PLS approach weights manifests variables into latent variables relative to their ability to predict the dependent variable(s) of interest. PLS-PM is often contrasted with alternative covariance-based structural equation modeling (CB-SEM) methods. As noted earlier, we provide some additional output for the PLS-PM we estimate here in the appendix. For much more on the PLS-PM method than we are able to provide here, including its many differences with CB-SEM, see: W. W. Chin, J. Henseler, and H. Wang (Eds.). 2010. *Handbook of Partial Least Squares* (Heidelberg: Springer).

15. Another useful feature of SEM is the ability to calculate both direct and "total" effects, which are the sum product of any independent variable's both direct and indirect effects on a dependent variable. But again, in the interest of simplicity, we will not discuss total effects here.

5 Using Citizen Satisfaction Results: A Multidimensional Priority Matrix Approach for Satisfaction Improvement

1. A search of the academic literature reveals the first mention of a "priority matrix" in a 1962 paper on a "multi computer command-and-control" system being developed for military applications, although the term may very well predate the early 1960s.

2. For an additional, and slightly more complex perspective on the priority matrix, see: J. Lewis. 2007. *The Project Manager's Desk Reference* (New York: McGraw Hill). For a good application of this tool in a fashion not dissimilar to what we are doing here, see: C. C, Chen, C. S. Wu, and R. C. F. Wu. 2006. "E-Service Enhancement Priority Matrix: The Case of an IC Foundry Company." *Information & Management* 43(5): 572–586.

3. A simple example of how changes might occur that make some areas or activities "more important" over time is the IT or e-government revolution that has occurred within government over the past two decades. While 15 years ago the quality of a government website might have been a very low priority attribute in driving satisfaction, or a feature used by so few respondents as to be irrelevant, it has become much more important for most government agencies, a phenomenon we discussed to some extent in chapter 1, and something we look at more closely in chapter 6.

4. In this sample, a vast majority of the respondents to the survey who indicated experiencing VA's services were veterans or their relatives who had applied for and/or received either veteran's benefits from the Veterans Benefits Administration (VBA), or health benefits from the Veterans Health Administration (VHA). As such, we will treat this sample as benefits applicants and recipients, which will become important for our data and results interpretation later along.

5. Using this aggregation procedure, the smallest segment or subsample over the five-year period consists of about 300 interviews/responses (for Passport Services), while the two largest are almost 1,200 cases each (for the IRS and SSA).

6. An example of seasonality in this type of data—which is simply any regular periodic fluctuation in results obtained via data that suggests the data is time-dependent—might be seen for the IRS. While the IRS is "in business" all year long, immediately before, during and after tax season is the agency's busiest time, and a time when citizens' feelings about the agency are most likely more acute, one way or another. Furthermore, noteworthy events (such as a massive system failure, a government shutdown, etc.) could impact satisfaction results, and if some data was collected during or immediately after such an event, while some was not, comparing results could become more difficult.

7. As mentioned briefly in chapters 3 and 4, it is important to examine somewhat generic, universal factors when conducting this kind of cross-agency satisfaction modeling, as one of our primary goals is to reach across and compare agencies and programs that may offer very different services and experiences to citizens. But as we hope becomes clear in the exercises we pursue in this chapter, if we were to attempt to examine a set of unique factors for each agency or program—attributes that drive satisfaction in a specific but non-generalizable way for that particular program—then our ability to benchmark and compare would be severely limited. While individual programs/agencies may very well need to "drill-down" into these kinds of activities at some point during a research project similar to this one, such data is often difficult (or impossible) to benchmark across agencies accurately.

8. One of the more difficult decisions in designing this kind of matrix, oddly enough, is where to set the upper and lower bounds on the two axes, and this is something that itself needs to be done carefully. For this matrix, we have established reasonable bounds based on the best/worst, most/least important scores for VA. But as you can see, even small changes in the range of either of the axes could lead to substantially different conclusions.

9. For three examples of recent research benchmarking citizen satisfaction data, see: F. V. Morgeson III. 2011. "Comparing Determinants of Website Satisfaction and Loyalty across the e-Government and e-Business Domains." *Electronic Government: An International Journal* 8(2/3): 164–184; F. V. Morgeson III and S. Mithas. 2009. "Does E-Government Measure Up to E-Business? Comparing End-user Perceptions of U.S. Federal Government and E-Business Websites." *Public Administration Review* 69(4): 740–52; F. V. Morgeson III and C. Petrescu 2011. "Do They All Perform Alike? An Examination of Perceived Performance, Citizen Satisfaction and Trust with U.S. Federal Agencies." *International Review of Administrative Sciences* 77(3): 451–479.

10. For evidence of this "age effect," see: B. E. Bryant and J. Cha. 1996. "Crossing the Threshold: Some Customers Are Harder to Please Than Others." *Marketing Research* 8(4): 21–28.

11. Indeed, increasingly in many countries, including the United States (where the OMB has been given the job), a single central government unit is tasked with creating and managing a government-wide performance measurement strategy, providing evidence that central governments have grown more interested in this type of system-wide performance improvement.

12. Technically, what we do in the priority matrix in figure 5.5 is impossible, in that we attempt to display 3 dimensions (Citizen Satisfaction, Trust, and # of Citizen-Users) in a two-dimensional graph. One fairly easy solution to this would have been to create an interactive term that combines Trust and # of Citizen-Users, perhaps by multiplying the two. But for our somewhat more limited explanatory purposes here, we will treat these three dimensions two-dimensionally, so that the matrix and data are more easily understood.

13. Perhaps not surprisingly, given our findings concerning the importance of improvements with the IRS, the recently passed H.R. 1660, the pending government customer service improvement act discussed in chapter 1, will mandate (if passed into law) that three agencies be included in the pilot program: the IRS, and two other agencies to be determined by Congress later.

6 Enduring Lessons in Citizen Satisfaction: Trends, Findings, and Public-Private Comparisons

1. The data used here includes five years of results only, but earlier findings—including the gap between the public and private sectors, but really all of the lessons discussed in this chapter—are highly consistent. For the private sector, the customer satisfaction score is based on results

from an ACSI study of more than 40 economic industries covering approximately one-third of US gross domestic product, derived from roughly 60,000 interviews of consumers each year. The federal government data is derived from an annual ACSI study of 1,500 respondents asked about their experiences with any federal government program/agency/department they have experienced (the data examined in a slightly different fashion in chapters 4 and 5), while the local government data includes results from approximately 1,000 annual interviews of consumers (both urban and suburban) about their satisfaction with certain core, ubiquitous services offered at this level (police, waste disposal, etc.).

2. For the best known, classic example of the argument linking consumer utility (or satisfaction) to competition, see: Adam Smith. 1776. *The Wealth of Nations* (London, England: Penguin Books).

3. For a discussion of the complexity of the transfer of government services to private sector control, see: S. Cohen. 2001. "A Strategic Framework for Devolving Responsibility and Functions from Government to the Private Sector." *Public Administration Review* 61(4): 432–440.

4. While due to space limitations we do not reproduce the full list of ACSI e-government scores analyzed here, all of the individual federal website satisfaction scores are publicly available and can be viewed on ACSI's website at: www.theacsi.org.

5. Further evidence of this phenomenon was provided in chapter 5. In the program-level data investigated there, we also saw a substantial range between the worst-performing agency examined (the IRS at 57) and the best (the NPS at 80).

6. For a discussion of these issues, particularly as they pertain to e-government, see: K. Layne and J. Lee. 2001. "Developing Fully Functional E-Government: A Four Stage Model." *Government Information Quarterly* 18(2): 122–36.

7. For a review of this phenomenon, see: D. F. Kettl. 2000. *The Global Public Management Revolution: A Report on the Transformation of Governance* (Washington, DC: Brookings Institution Press).

8. To avoid confusion, the data displayed in figure 6.3 comes from a study examining just citizen experiences with VHA's inpatient and outpatient hospital services, not with the VA or VHA application processes as a whole, like the sample investigated in chapter 5. The difference provides a good example of variance in satisfaction performance across types of government experience; in this case, it shows that benefits applicants are generally less satisfied than those already receiving benefits (in this case, as patients at a VA hospital).

9. For those skeptical of the VHA's performance, a variety of commentators have pointed to these hospital's improved performance over the last few years, and how these improvements have slowly begun to "shakeoff" the negative images embedded in American's minds following the Vietnam War. For examples, see: C. J. Gearon. "Military Might: Today's VA Hospitals Are Models of Top-Notch Care." *US News & World Report*. July 18, 2005; D. Stires. "How the VA Healed Itself." *Fortune*. May 15, 2006.

10. For some examples of this model as it has been applied to the public sector, see: F. V. Morgeson III. 2013. "Expectations, Disconfirmation and Citizen Satisfaction with the U.S. Federal Government: Testing and Expanding the Model." *Journal of Public Administration Research and Theory* 23(2): 289–305; G. G. Van Ryzin. 2006. "Testing the Expectancy Disconfirmation Model of Citizen Satisfaction with Local Government." *Journal of Public Administration Research and Theory* (16)4: 599–611.

11. One widely accepted measure of e-government development is the UN's "E-Government Development Index" and its "E-Government Readiness Index." For more information on these studies, see: http://unpan3.un.org/egovkb/index.aspx.

12. For this claim, see: G. Nagesh. "OMB Touts Savings from E-gov Initiatives." *GovExec.com*. February 7, 2008. Accessed online at: www.govexec.com/dailyfed/0208/020708n1.htm.

13. One difference between the results presented here and those offered in lesson #2 is the data included in the averages. While the data in lesson #2 includes all measures for 2011, and results in an annual average of 75.4, the results offered here include only websites measured during Q4, and used as a year-on-year average satisfaction score for each website, explaining the difference between the two scores.

14. For example, see: F. V. Morgeson III and S. Mithas. 2009. "Does E-Government Measure up to E-Business? Comparing End-User Perceptions of US Federal Government and E-Business Web sites." *Public Administration Review* 69(4): 740–52.

15. As the "finishing touches" were being put on this book in the fall of 2013, the US federal government's HealthCare.gov website was launched (the website mostly responsible for implementing the entire Affordable Care Act and the new health insurance marketplace), with results and a public reception that most would regard as disastrous.

16. For the year 2012, one news source indicated that the IRS suggested that it would only be able to "answer 68% of its calls and a disappointing 48% of written correspondences within established time frames." While for the IRS this is caused mostly by small budgets limiting the

size of call center staff, it serves to discourage citizens from complaining at all. K. P. Erb. "Congress Threatens IRS With 'Right-Sized' Budget Cuts." *Forbes.com*. July 14, 2013. Accessed online at: www.forbes.com /sites/kellyphillipserb/2013/07/14/congress-threatens-irs-with-right-sized -budget-cuts/.

17. For the results of this study, visit the Pew Web site at: www.people-press. org/2010/04/18/section-1-trust-in-government-1958–2010/.

18. For just a few examples of this complex phenomenon, see: C. W. Thomas. 1998. "Maintaining and Restoring Public Trust In Government Agencies and Their Employees." *Administration & Society* 30(2): 166–193; S. Van de Walle and G. Bouckaert, G. 2003. "Public Service Performance and Trust in Government: The Problem of Causality." *International Journal of Public Administration* 29(8–9): 891–913.

19. J. Chait. "Partisanship And Declining Trust In Government." *The New Republic*. April 11, 2011; M. J. Hetherington. 1998. "The Political Relevance of Political Trust." *American Political Science Review* 92(4): 791–808.

20. R. D. Putnam. 2000. *Bowling Alone: The Collapse and Revival of American Community* (New York: Simon & Schuster).

21. J. Habermas. 1975. *Legitimation Crisis*, trans. Thomas McCarthy (Boston, MA: Beacon Press).

22. Van de Walle and Bouckaert, G. "Public Service Performance and Trust in Government," 891–913.

7   Governing in an Age of Scarcity: On the Role of Cross-National Citizen Satisfaction Measurement

1. For an excellent—albeit somewhat early—review of the events surrounding the Arab Spring, see: L. Noueihed and A. Warren. 2012. *The Battle for the Arab Spring: Revolution, Counter-Revolution and the Making of a New Era* (New Haven, CT: Yale University Press).

2. While we may never know for certain, recent estimates have suggested that Muammar Gaddafi died the richest person on the planet, and quite possibly *the richest person to ever live*, with a total fortune over $200 billion, although there is some debate on what assets truly belonged to Gaddafi (if any), and what were rightfully assets of the Libyan nation. See: E. Durgy. "Did Moammar Gadhafi Die the Richest Man in the World?" *Forbes*. October 25, 2011.

3. Another relevant cause, one that we haven't the space or time to consider fully here, was the rapid proliferation of digital media throughout the Arab world in the early 2000s. The information and communications

technology revolution, which we discussed briefly in chapter 1, and innovations like social media played a major role in the 2009 protests in Iran, as well as the Arab Spring revolts that followed. Not only did IT allow citizens in these countries to communicate with one another, share information, and coordinate actions and protests against the state, but it also allowed many people to gain a better understanding of conditions in the West and the more-developed world, and to see the advantages citizens in these countries enjoyed.

4. From 2003 to 2008, the price of oil (per barrel) had increased quickly, spurred by wars in the Middle East and increased consumer demand. In the summer of 2008, the price of crude oil had spiked at an all-time high of more than $145 per barrel. This boon in cash had padded the coffers of the governing powers in these states, and had allowed them to weather the increases in food prices and to give slightly more of the largesse to their societies in the years prior, via more and better-paying state jobs. But as a consequence of the global economic slowdown (and reversal) caused by the Great Recession, these record-high oil prices vanished almost overnight. Between July and December of 2008, oil dropped from $145 per barrel to just over $30 per barrel, drastically impacting the financial capabilities of many of these regimes.

5. As one author nicely summarizes the incompetence of these governments prior to the Arab Spring: "But in the Arab autocracies, the poor, the working classes, and the middle classes met only callous indifference, corruption, and humiliation when they sought redress from their governments. Indeed, the *massive, bloated, corrupt government bureaucracies did nothing to alleviate the suffering of their people and a great deal to make it more painful*" [my italics]. K. M. Pollack. 2011. *The Arab Awakening: America and the Transformation of the Middle East* (Washington, DC: The Brookings Institution).

6. All of the population projection data provided here comes from the United Nations Department of Economic and Social Affairs, Population Estimates and Projections Section. The data can be accessed at their website: www.un.org/esa/population/unpop.htm.

7. For instance, according to "The Economist" and their "Global Debt Clock," global government debt doubled between just 2004 and 2012. See: www.economist.com/content/global_debt_clock.

8. For a nice description of the causes and consequences of demographic "graying," see: C. Freeland. "The Problems of a Graying Population." *New York Times*. July 28, 2011.

9. While the above thoughts on the impact of population growth and governmental resources may seem pessimistic, one of the oldest theories

of the impact of population growth shared this pessimism, specifically arguing that basic resources (such as food and water) could not keep up with rapid population expansion. T. R. Malthus. 2007. *An Essay on the Principle of Population* (Mineola, NY: Dover Publications).

10. A popular body of research points to the existence of a "youth bulge," where a nation has a large proportion of its population in the younger age groups (teens and twenties), as a major factor in explaining social and political instability. For an example, see: H. Urdal. 2006. "A Clash of Generations? Youth Bulges and Political Violence." *International Studies Quarterly* 50(3): 607–629.

11. For example, see: World Economic Forum. 2011. "The Future of Government: Lessons Learned from around the World." Available online at: www3.weforum.org/docs/EU11/WEF_EU11_FutureofGovernment_Report.pdf.

12. For just one example, see: V. Kumar. 1999. *International Marketing Research* (Upper Saddle River, NJ: Prentice Hall).

13. For a review of many of these issues, see: J. A. Harkness, F. de Vijver, and P. Mohler (Eds.). 2003. *Cross-Cultural Survey Methods* (Hoboken, NJ: John Wiley & Sons).

14. For just a few of the many, many works linking customer satisfaction to financial performance, see: L. Aksoy et al. 2008. "The Long-Term Stock Market Valuation of Customer Satisfaction." *Journal of Marketing* 72(4): 105–122; C. Fornell et al. 2006. "Customer Satisfaction and Stock Prices: High Returns, Low Risk." *Journal of Marketing* 70(1): 1–14.

Appendix

1. For much more on PLS-PM than we are able to provide here, see: V. E. Vinzi, L. Trinchera, and S. Amato. 2010. "PLS Path Modeling: From Foundations to Recent Developments and Open Issues for Model Assessment and Improvement," in *Handbook of Partial Least Squares*, W.W. Chin, J. Henseler and H. Wang (eds.) (Heidelberg: Springer).

2. To keep the model a little less cluttered, we do not include all of the error terms for each of the manifest variables within the latent variables, but this is often included in a graphic structural equation model as well.

3. In reality, Complaint Rate, Confidence, and Overall Trust are not endogenous *latent* variables in the model we have estimated here, but rather endogenous *observed* variables. Likewise, the exogenous Expectations variable is an observed variable as well, not a latent variable. This is because each contains only a single survey variable, unlike

Citizen Satisfaction and the three latent exogenous latent variables (Information, Process, and Customer Service). Nevertheless, in many models these variables will or could be multivariate latent variables, and could have been modeled as latent variables here (with the inclusion of additional observed variables to our model), and so we treat the model as though all variables were latent variables to (hopefully) make the LISREL notation a little less confusing.

4. While we won't discuss them more here, the other pieces of data are a bootstrapped (or resampled) version of the GoF ("GoF Boot."), the standard error of the GoF, the critical value (similar to a t-value in regression), and the upper and lower bounds of the GoF estimates.

Bibliography

Ackerman, J. M. and I. E. Sandoval-Ballesteros. 2006. "The Global Explosion of Freedom of Information Laws." *Administrative Law Review* 58(1): 85–130.

Aksoy, L., B. Cooil, C. Groening, T. Keiningham, and A. Yalcin. 2008. "The Long-Term Stock Market Valuation of Customer Satisfaction." *Journal of Marketing* 72(4): 105–122.

Allison, P. D. 1999. *Multiple Regression: A Primer.* Thousand Oaks, CA: Pine Forge Press.

Anderson, C. J. and C. A. Guillory. 1997. "Political Institutions and Satisfaction with Democracy: A Cross-National Analysis of Consensus and Majoritarian Systems." *American Political Science Review* 91(1): 66–81.

Berry, William D. 1993. *Understanding Regression Assumptions.* Newbury Park, CA: Sage Publications.

Bollen, K. A. 1989. *Structural Equations with Latent Variables.* New York: John Wiley & Sons.

Bouckaert, G. and S. Van de Walle. 2003. "Comparing Measures of Citizen Trust and User Satisfaction as Indicators of "Good Governance." *International Review of Administrative Sciences* 69(3): 329–343.

Box, R. 1999. "Running Government like a Business: Implications for Public Administration Theory and Practice." *American Review of Public Administration* 29(1): 19–43.

Boxwell, R. J. 1994. *Benchmarking for Competitive Advantage.* New York: McGraw Hill.

Bryant, B. E. and J. Cha. 1996. "Crossing the Threshold: Some Customers Are Harder to Please Than Others." *Marketing Research* 8(4): 21–28.

Cardozo, R. N. 1965. "An Experimental Study of Customer Effort, Expectation, and Satisfaction." *Journal of Marketing Research* 2(3): 244–249.

Chait, J. "Partisanship and Declining Trust in Government." *The New Republic.* April 11, 2011.

Chen, C. C., C. S. Wu, and R. C. F. Wu. 2006. "E-Service Enhancement Priority Matrix: The Case of an IC Foundry Company." *Information & Management* 43(5): 572–586.

Chief Financial Officers Act of 1990, Pub. L. No. 101–576.

Chin, W. W. 2010. "How to Write Up and Report PLS Analyses." In *Handbook of Partial Least Squares*, W. W. Chin, J. Henseler, and H. Wang (Eds.). Heidelberg: Springer.

Chin, W. W., J. Henseler, and H. Wang (Eds.). 2010. *Handbook of Partial Least Squares*. Heidelberg: Springer.

Cohen, S. 2001. "A Strategic Framework for Devolving Responsibility and Functions from Government to the Private Sector." *Public Administration Review* 61(4): 432–440.

Cole, R. L. 1975. "Citizen Participation in Municipal Politics." *American Journal of Political Science* 19(4): 761–781.

Cook, B. J. 1996. *Bureaucracy and Self-Government: Reconsidering the Role of Public Administration in American Politics*. Baltimore, MD: Johns Hopkins University Press.

Cusack, T. R. 1999. "The Shaping of Popular Satisfaction with Government and Regime Performance in Germany." *British Journal of Political Science* 29: 641–672.

Diener, E. D., R. A. Emmons, R. J. Larsen, and S. Griffin. 1985. "The Satisfaction with Life Scale." *Journal of Personality Assessment* 49(1): 71–75.

Durgy, E. "Did Moammar Gadhafi Die the Richest Man in the World?" *Forbes*. October 25, 2011.

E-Government Act of 2002, Pub. L. No. 107–347.

Enders, C. K. 2010. *Applied Missing Data Analysis*. New York: The Guilford Press.

Erb, K. P. "Congress Threatens IRS with "Right-Sized" Budget Cuts." *Forbes.com*. July 14, 2013. Accessed online at: www.forbes.com/sites /kellyphillipserb/2013/07/14/congress-threatens-irs-with-right-sized-budget -cuts/.

Evans, D. 1999. "Congress, Oversight and the Diversity of Member Goals." *Political Science Quarterly* 109(4): 669–687.

Exec. Order No. 13,450, 72 Fed. Reg. 64519.

Exec. Order No. 13,571, 76 Fed. Reg. 24339.

Federal Financial Management Improvement Act of 1996, Pub. L. No. 104–208.

Fornell, C. 1992. "A National Customer Satisfaction Barometer: The Swedish Experience." *The Journal of Marketing* 56(1): 6–21.

———. 2007. *The Satisfied Customer: Winners and Losers in the Battle for Buyer Preference*. New York: Palgrave Macmillan.

Fornell, C., S. Mithas, F. V. Morgeson III, and M. S. Krishan. 2006. "Customer Satisfaction and Stock Prices: High Returns, Low Risk." *Journal of Marketing* 70(1): 1–14.

The Freedom of Information Act of 1966, Pub. L. No. 89–487.

Gearon, C. J. "Military Might: Today's VA Hospitals Are Models of Top-Notch Care." *U.S. News & World Report*. July 18, 2005.

Government Customer Service Improvement Act of 2013 (H.R. 1660).

Government Management Reform Act of 1994, Pub. L. No. 103–356.

Government Performance and Results Act of 1993, Pub. L. No. 103–162.

Government Performance and Results Modernization Act of 2010, Pub. L. No. 111–352.

Gutmann, A. and D. Thompson. 1996. *Democracy and Disagreement.* Cambridge, MA: The Belknap Press of Harvard University.

Habermas, J. 1975. *Legitimation Crisis.* Trans. by Thomas McCarthy. Boston, MA: Beacon Press.

Harkness, J. A., F. de Vijver, and P. Mohler (Eds.) 2003. *Cross-Cultural Survey Methods.* Hoboken, NJ: John Wiley & Sons.

Hatry, H. P. 1972. "Issues in Productivity Measurement for Local Governments." *Public Administration Review* 32(6): 776–784.

———. 2006. *Performance Measurement: Getting Results.* Washington, DC: Urban Institute Press.

Hatry, H. P., J. E. Marcotte, T. Van Houten, and C. H. Weiss. 1998. *Customer Surveys for Agency Managers: What Managers Need to Know.* Washington, DC: The Urban Institute Press.

Hetherington, M. J. 1998. "The Political Relevance of Political Trust." *American Political Science Review* 92(4): 791–808.

Hirschman, A. O. 1970. *Exit, Voice and Loyalty: Responses to Declines in Firms, Organizations and States.* Cambridge, MA: Harvard University Press.

Homer-Dixon, T. F. 1999. *The Environment, Scarcity, and Violence.* Princeton, NJ: Princeton University Press.

Hoppock, R. and C. L. Odom. 1940. "Job Satisfaction." *Occupations: The Vocational Guidance Journal* 19(1): 24–29.

Hotchkiss, G. B. 1925. "An Economic Defence of Advertising." *The American Economic Review* 15(1): 14–22.

Hulland, J., M. J. Ryan, and R. K. Rayner. 2010. "Modeling Customer Satisfaction: A Comparative Performance Evaluation of Covariance Structure Analysis Versus Partial Least Squares." In *Handbook of Partial Least Squares*, W.W. Chin, J. Henseler and H. Wang (Eds.). Heidelberg: Springer.

Information Technology Management Reform Act of 1996, Pub. L. No. 104–106.

Jones, L. R. and F. Thompson. 1999. *Public Management: Institutional Renewal for the Twenty-First Century.* Stamford, CT: JAI Press.

Jones, L. R. and J. L. McCaffery. 1992. "Federal Financial Management Reform and the Chief Financial Officers Act." *Public Budgeting and Finance* 12(4): 75–86.

Kaboolian, L. 1998. "The New Public Management: Challenging the Boundaries of the Administration vs. Management Debate." *Public Administration Review* 58(3): 189–193.

Keehley, P. S., S. Medlin, S. McBride, and L. Longmire. 1997. *Benchmarking for Best Practices in the Public Sector: Achieving Performance Breakthroughs in Federal, State, and Local Agencies.* San Francisco, CA: Jossey-Bass.

Kelly, J. and D. Swindell. 2002. "A Multiple Indicator Approach to Municipal Service Evaluation: Correlating Performance and Citizen Satisfaction across Jurisdictions." *Public Administration Review* 62(5): 610–621.

Kettl, D. F. 2000. *The Global Public Management Revolution: A Report on the Transformation of Governance.* Washington, DC: Brookings Institution Press.

Kouzmin, A., E. Loffler, H. Klages, and N. Kakabadse. 1999. "Benchmarking and Performance Measurement in Public Sectors." *International Journal of Public Sector Management* 12(2): 121–144.

Kravchuk, R. S. and R. W. Schack. 1996. "Designing Effective Performance-Measurement Systems under the Government Performance and Results Act of 1993." *Public Administration Review* 56(4): 348–358.

Kumar, V. 1999. *International Marketing Research.* Upper Saddle River, NJ: Prentice Hall.

Layne, K. and J. Lee. 2001. "Developing Fully Functional E-Government: A Four Stage Model." *Government Information Quarterly* 18(2): 122–136.

Lewis, B. W. 1938. "The 'Consumer' and 'Public' Interests under Public Regulation." *The Journal of Political Economy* 46(1): 97–107.

Lewis, J. 2007. *The Project Manager's Desk Reference.* New York: McGraw Hill.

Lowi, T. J. 1969. *The End of Liberalism: The Second Republic of the United States.* New York: W. W. Norton.

Malthus, T. R. 2007. *An Essay on the Principle of Population.* Mineola, NY: Dover Publications.

Marsden, P. V. and J. D. Wright (Eds.). 2010. *Handbook of Survey Research.* 2nd Edition. UK: Emerald Group Publishing.

Melkers, J. and K. Willoughby. 1998. "The State of the States: Performance-Based Budgeting Requirements in 47 out of 50." *Public Administration Review* 58(1): 66–73.

Mithas, S. 2011. *Digital Intelligence: What Every Smart Manager Must Have for Success in an Information Age.* North Potomac, MD: Finerplanet.

Morgan, N. A. and L. L. Rego. 2006. "The Value of Different Customer Satisfaction and Loyalty Metrics in Predicting Business Performance." *Marketing Science* 25(5): 426–439.

Morgeson III, F. V. 2005. *Reconciling Democracy and Bureaucracy: Towards a Deliberative-Democratic Model of Bureaucratic Accountability.* PhD Dissertation, University of Pittsburgh.

———. 2011. "Comparing Determinants of Website Satisfaction and Loyalty across the E-Government and E-Business Domains." *Electronic Government: An International Journal* 8(2/3): 164–184.

———. 2013. "Expectations, Disconfirmation, and Citizen Satisfaction with the US Federal Government: Testing and Expanding the Model." *Journal of Public Administration Research and Theory* 23(2): 289–305.

Morgeson III, F. V. and C. Petrescu. 2011. "Do They All Perform Alike? An Examination of Perceived Performance, Citizen Satisfaction and Trust with U.S. Federal Agencies." *International Review of Administrative Sciences* 77(3): 451–479.

Morgeson III, F. V. and S. Mithas. 2009. "Does E-Government measure up to E-Business? Comparing End-user Perceptions of U.S. Federal Government and E-Business Websites." *Public Administration Review* 69(4): 740–752.

Morgeson III, F. V., D. VanAmburg, and S. Mithas. 2011. "Misplaced Trust? Exploring the Structure of the E-Government-Citizen Trust Relationship." *Journal of Public Administration Research and Theory* 21(2): 257–283.

Mueller, R. O. 1995. *Basic Principles of Structural Equation Modeling: An Introduction to LISREL and EQS*. New York: Springer.

Nagesh, G. "OMB Touts Savings from E-gov Initiatives." *GovExec.com*. February 7, 2008. Accessed online at: www.govexec.com/dailyfed/0208/020708n1.htm.

Noueihed, L. and A. Warren. 2012. *The Battle for the Arab Spring: Revolution, Counter-Revolution and the Making of a New Era*. New Haven, CT: Yale University Press.

Oliver, R. L. 1980. "A Cognitive Model of the Antecedents and Consequences of Satisfaction Decisions." *Journal of Marketing Research* 17(4): 460–469.

———. 2010. *Satisfaction: A Behavioral Perspective on the Consumer*. New York: ME Sharpe Incorporated.

Olsen, L. L. and M. D. Johnson. 2003. "Service Equity, Satisfaction, and Loyalty: From Transaction-Specific to Cumulative Evaluations." *Journal of Service Research* 5(3): 184–195.

Oppenheim, A. N. 1992. *Questionnaire Design, Interviewing and Attitude Measurement*. 3rd Edition. New York: Continuum Publishing.

O'Shaughnessy, N. J. and S. C. Henneberg, (Eds.). 2002. *The Idea of Political Marketing*. Westport, CT: Greenwood Publishing Group.

Ostrom, E., R. B. Parks, and G. P. Whitaker. 1973. "Do We Really Want to Consolidate Urban Police Forces? A Reappraisal of Some Old Assertions." *Public Administration Review* 33(5): 423–432.

Ostrom, E., R. B. Parks, S. L. Percy, and G. P. Whitaker. 1979. "Evaluating Police Organization." *Public Productivity Review* 3(3): 3–27.

Park, H. and J. Blenkinsopp. 2011. "The Roles of Transparency and Trust in the Relationship between Corruption and Citizen Satisfaction." *International Review of Administrative Sciences* 77 (2): 254–274.

Peters, B. G. 2001. *The Politics of Bureaucracy*. London, UK: Routledge.

Pharr, S. J. and R. D. Putnam (Eds.) 2000. *Disaffected Democracies: What's Troubling the Trilateral Countries?* Princeton, NJ: Princeton University Press.

Phillips, C. F. 1941. "A Critical Analysis of Recent Literature Dealing with Marketing Efficiency." *The Journal of Marketing* 5(4): 360–365.

Poister, T. H. and J. C. Thomas. 2011. "The Effect of Expectations and Expectancy Confirmation/Disconfirmation on Motorists' Satisfaction with State Highways." *Journal of Public Administration Research and Theory* 21(4): 601–617.

Pollack, K. M. 2011. *The Arab Awakening: America and the Transformation of the Middle East.* Washington, DC: The Brookings Institution.

Putnam, R. D. 2000. *Bowling Alone: The Collapse and Revival of American Community.* New York: Simon & Schuster.

Radin, B. A. 1998. "The Government Performance and Results Act (GPRA): Hydra-Headed Monster or Flexible Management Tool?" *Public Administration Review* 58(4): 307–316.

Reddick, C. G. and J. Roy. 2012. "Business Perceptions and Satisfaction with E-Government: Findings from a Canadian Survey." *Government Information Quarterly* 30(1): 1–9.

Rezabakhsh, B., D. Bornemann, U. Hansen, and U. Schrader. 2006. "Consumer Power: A Comparison of the Old Economy and the Internet Economy." *Journal of Consumer Policy* 29(1): 3–36.

Scheaffer, R. L., W. Mendenhall III, R. L. Ott, and K. G. Gerow. 2012. *Elementary Survey Sampling.* 3rd Edition. Boston, MA: Cengage Learning.

Scitovsky, T. 1992. *The Joyless Economy: The Psychology of Human Satisfaction.* New York: Oxford University Press.

Serra, G. 1995. "Citizen-Initiated Contact and Satisfaction with Bureaucracy: A Multivariate Analysis." *Journal of Public Administration Research and Theory* 5(2): 175–188.

Sheskin, D. J. 2004. *Handbook of Parametric and Nonparametric Statistical Procedures.* 3rd Edition. Boca Raton, FL: CRC Press.

Simon, H. A. 1947. *Administrative Behavior.* New York: Free Press.

———. 1952. "A Comparison of Organisation Theories." *The Review of Economic Studies* 20(1): 40–48.

Smith, Adam. 1776. *The Wealth of Nations.* London, UK: Penguin Books.

Spector, A. J. 1956. "Expectations, Fulfillment, and Morale." *The Journal of Abnormal and Social Psychology* 52(1): 51–56.

Squire, P. 1988. "Why the 1936 Literary Digest Poll Failed." *Public Opinion Quarterly* 52 (1): 125–133.

Stagner, R. 1970. "Perceptions, Aspirations, Frustrations, and Satisfactions: An Approach to Urban Indicators." *The ANNALS of the American Academy of Political and Social Science* 388(1): 59–68.

Stalebrink, O. J. 2009. "National Performance Mandates and Intergovernmental Collaboration An Examination of the Program Assessment Rating Tool (PART)." *The American Review of Public Administration* 39(6): 619–639.

Stipak, B. 1979. "Citizen Satisfaction with Urban Services: Potential Misuse as a Performance Indicator." *Public Administration Review* 39(1): 46–52.

Stires, D. "How the VA Healed Itself." *Fortune.* May 15, 2006.

Strong, E. K. 1925. "Theories of Selling." *Journal of Applied Psychology* 9(1): 75–86.

Super, D. E. 1939. "Occupational Level and Job Satisfaction." *Journal of Applied Psychology* 23(5): 547–564.

Thomas, Craig W. 1998. "Maintaining and Restoring Public Trust in Government Agencies and their Employees." *Administration & Society* 30(2): 166–193.

Urdal, H. 2006. "A Clash of Generations? Youth Bulges and Political Violence." *International Studies Quarterly* 50(3): 607–629.

Van de Walle, S. and G. Bouckaert, G. 2003. "Public Service Performance and Trust in Government: The Problem of Causality." *International Journal of Public Administration* 29(8–9): 891–913.

Van Ryzin, G.G. 2006. "Testing the Expectancy Disconfirmation Model of Citizen Satisfaction with Local Government." *Journal of Public Administration Research and Theory* (16)4: 599–611.

———. 2007. "Pieces of a Puzzle: Linking Government Performance, Citizen Satisfaction and Trust." *Public Performance & Management Review* 30(4): 521–535.

Van Ryzin, G. G. and E. W. Freeman. 1997. "Viewing Organizations as Customers of Government Services: Data from Maryland's Housing Development Programs." *Public Productivity & Management Review* 20(4): 419–431.

Van Ryzin, G. G., D. Muzzio, S. Immerwahr, L. Gulick and E. Martinez. 2004. "Drivers and Consequences of Citizen Satisfaction: An Application of the American Customer Satisfaction Index Model to New York City." *Public Administration Review* 64(3): 331–341.

Vilares, M. J., M. H. Almeida, and P. S. Coelho. 2010. "Comparison of Likelihood and PLS Estimators for Structural Equation Modeling: A Simulation with Customer Satisfaction Data." In *Handbook of Partial Least Squares.* W. W. Chin, J. Henseler and H. Wang (Eds.). Heidelberg: Springer.

Vinzi, V. E., L. Trinchera, and S. Amato. 2010. "PLS Path Modeling: From Foundations to Recent Developments and Open Issues for Model Assessment and Improvement." In *Handbook of Partial Least Squares,* W. W. Chin, J. Henseler and H. Wang (Eds.). Heidelberg: Springer.

Wagenheim, G. D. and J. H. Reurink. 1991. "Customer Service in Public Administration." *Public Administration Review* 51(3): 263–270.

Warner, M. E. 2010. "The Future of Local Government: Twenty-First-Century Challenges." *Public Administration Review* 70(6): 145–147.

Warren, M. 1999. "Introduction." In *Democracy and Trust*, Mark Warren (Ed.). UK: Cambridge University Press.

Wilson, J. Q. 1989. *Bureaucracy: What Government Agencies Do and Why They Do It*. New York: Basic Books, Inc.

Wood, V., M. L. Wylie, and B. Sheafor. 1969. "An Analysis of a Short Self-Report Measure of Life Satisfaction: Correlation with Rater Judgments." *Journal of Gerontology* 24(4): 465–469.

World Economic Forum. 2011. "The Future of Government: Lessons Learned from Around the World." Available online at: www3.weforum.org/docs /EU11/WEF_EU11_FutureofGovernment_Report.pdf.

Wright, S. 1921. "Correlation and Causation." *Journal of Agricultural Research* XX(7): 557–587.

Yi, Y. 1990. "A Critical Review of Consumer Satisfaction." *Review of Marketing* 4(1): 68–123.

Index

Printed in the United States of America